D0866941

Reading to go places!

THIS GIFT PRESENTED TO:

_____

FROM

_____

WEALTH CONUNDRUM

A MONEY MANAGER WRESTLES WITH THE PUZZLES OF WEALTH

*CONUNDRUM (n) a problem where
the answer is very complex, possibly
unsolvable without deep investigation*

RALPH DOUDERA

Signature Editions
Atlanta, Georgia

Cover portrait of Ralph Doudera by Joseph Lust
Mother Teresa portrait on page 62 by Larry Braak

PUBLISHED BY SIGNATURE EDITIONS, 4875 Markim Forest Lane, Sugar Hill,
GA 30518, 678-714-0005   www.signature-editions.net

The following abbreviations are used to identify versions of the Bible in this book:

KJV *King James Version,* also known as the *Authorized Version.*

NKJV New King James Version. Copyright © 1982 by Thomas Nelson, Inc.
Used by permission. All rights reserved.

The Message *The Message, The Bible in Contemporary Language,* by Eugene H. Peterson.
Scripture quotes from *The Message* Copyright © 1993, 1994, 1995, 1996, 2000, 2001,
2002. Used by permission of NavPress Publishing Group. All rights reserved.

NLT Holy Bible New Living Translation, copyright © 1996 Tyndale Charitable Trust.
Used by permission of Tyndale House Publishers, Inc., Wheaton, Illinois 60189.
All rights reserved.

TLB The Living Bible © 1971 by Tyndale House Publishers, Wheaton, Illinois.

Nouns and pronouns referring to deity are capitalized throughout the text of this
book unless they are included within a direct quotation, in which case the original
capitalization is retained.

Includes bibliographical references.
ISBN: 0-9776892-0-4
Library of Congress Control Number: 2005938550

Design: The DesignWorks Group; cover, Wes Youssi; interior, Robin Black,
        www.thedesignworksgroup.com

Printed in the United States of America
First Printing January 2006

DEDICATION

*With gratitude to a God Who has given me all I am,
I dedicate this book to my children,
SCOTT, ERIN, LAURA, ELIZABETH,
RACHEL, and JESSIE,
who have revealed to me what true wealth is.
May the lessons I have learned bear fruit in your
families for generations to come.*

*And thank you TARA, for your non-stop
encouragement on the most challenging and rewarding
project I have ever attempted.*

CONTENTS

EMOTIONAL CRASH

My money was managing me.

In later years, I would look back on Black Monday, October 19, 1987, as one of the low points of my life. It wasn't that I lost my money or my clients' money that day as the freefalling stock market had the largest one-day decline in history.

My money was safe. The week before, I had strategically shifted all of my funds into money markets.

It wasn't the lost money. It was the loss of control. It was the fear.

My mind went wild with anxiety all day long. What if the financial system of the world went into meltdown? What if the money market mutual funds were not safe after all? What would I do? When I went home, I was suffering such emotional burnout that I could hardly relate to my family, and I was certainly not being a good husband and father.

Unfortunately, it wasn't that unusual, either. My attitude at home was ruled by the whims of the market. Even when I had a good day and made money, I would still be upset and unreasonable with everyone. This money business was too much. I resolved to quit.

> I WAS ON SUCH AN EMOTIONAL ROLLER
> COASTER THAT I HAD TO STOP WATCHING
> THOSE GYRATING STOCK PRICES.
> I RESOLVED TO
> LOOK AT THEM JUST ONCE
> AT THE END OF THE DAY.

The crash seemed to confirm a decision I had made earlier to quit the money management business for good. In my mind I decided that I could find investment managers who seldom lost money. Let them make money for me. They could watch my treasure. Then my life would be void of problems. Right? A new start would be good, I thought. That was not exactly what happened.

I decided that I should just go on and retire as I had been planning to do for years. Even though I was only 40 years old, that was a legitimate option. I had made enough money to retire, but why did I seem to be turning out like all those unhappy rich people I met when I had been selling life insurance? What was wrong with me?

I LOVED MONEY.
AS LONG AS I COULD REMEMBER,
I HAD ALWAYS WANTED TO HAVE MONEY,
AND THAT WAS THE WAY
MY LIFE HAD TURNED OUT.

I didn't ever want to sell life insurance, but when it was either that or be broke, I found that it was extremely profitable. I learned to target old rich guys for my sales. I was told that I could make as much as the people who bought my policies, and that was what happened. After a while, I retired from the insurance and estate planning profession and went into money management. I always knew in the back of my mind that I had enough money so that I would never again have to ask anyone to buy an insurance policy or ask anyone for financial help. I was set for life. Or so I thought.

Theoretically, I never should have been in such a state of agitation as I was on that day when the market went down. I was a Christian. I thought that I had been taking steps toward letting God take control of my life ever since I was 23 and just finishing college. I went on a retreat as I was starting my new career as an engineer. I told God that I would give Him control of my life.

MY OFFER TO GOD EXCLUDED
TWO CAREER PATHS THAT I DIDN'T WANT TO
FOLLOW. I HAD HEARD TOO MANY STORIES
OF NICE PEOPLE BEING TOLD BY GOD TO GO
INTO THE JUNGLES OF AFRICA, AND I
DIDN'T WANT TO SELL INSURANCE, SO I PUT
THOSE CAREERS ON MY "NEVER" LIST.

Well, not total control. It was a little too scary to give God everything, since I like to control my own decisions, so I gave God a few exceptions. That seemed reasonable. I mean, who grows up and wants to do things like being a missionary or selling life insurance? No prestige, and certainly no money—and I wanted to make big bucks. However, three years later on another retreat I gave in and gave God those other options, and within six months I was selling life insurance. Oh well. Yes, God's got a sense of humor. But it actually turned out to be a real money maker.

I had put myself out there about making money way back when I graduated from high school, right in the Union High School yearbook. Under my name it listed my aspiration—"to be a highly paid engineer." Not a great engineer, mind you, not a notable one, but "show me the money." My mom, being a devout Baptist, was so disappointed when she read my comments that she asked me, "Why didn't you say what Diane in your Sunday School class wrote on her yearbook photo—'to do God's will'?"

"That's not what I want," I told her shortly. I loved money. That was the bottom line. Now look where it was leading me. Nowhere. Fast. She probably got a hint that I had a problem in this area when I was arrested at age 17 for shoplifting. Who would believe it—a tithing Baptist thief?

I was raised in an upper middle class home, and money was never really discussed all that much. It later seemed to me that we had a poverty complex about certain things. Maybe that philosophy was left over from the Depression years that my parents had lived through, but it seemed that as a family we were never able to buy anything unless it was on sale. We waited in bone-chilling lines in the middle of winter for the after-Christmas sales. We never threw anything away. Giving to a beggar was out of the question. We worked hard for our money and they could just get theirs the same way.

My grandfather was an active investor during the Depression, and I later found out that he had considered suicide when the stock market crashed. Was that where I was headed? Was this stuff hereditary? Why did I love money so much? What was it doing to me? How was it affecting the people in my life?

When I was in college, I was the only guy in my fraternity house who got the *Wall Street Journal*. I was always on the lookout for ways to get rich. I even took out a low interest student loan and invested the money in over-the-counter stocks. I didn't even have to think about it. I just knew that I wanted to get rich. After I graduated from college and went to work, my first employer put so much pressure on me for a United Way contribution that I almost lost my job over it. Seems like they were 100 percent participation except for me. Eventually I caved in, but only after a fight.

I NOT ONLY LOVED MONEY.
I WANTED TO HANG ONTO IT.
I NEVER GAVE ANYTHING TO ANYBODY.
WHY WAS I SO CHEAP?

I tried investing in stocks, bonds, commodities, gold, diamonds, oil drilling partnerships, numismatic coins and multilevel marketing. Solomon, one of the wealthiest and wisest men who ever lived said, "Whoever loves money never has money enough."[1] That was me, a lover of money!

I ASKED MYSELF,
CAN A CHRISTIAN HAVE WEALTH?

I needed help. A retreat conference called Camps Farthest Out (CFO) always seemed to have a conference somewhere at a time when I needed spiritual insight. After the crash, when I made the decision to retire and stop investing by giving my funds to someone else to invest, I took my Bible and went off to a CFO camp to get some new direction. It turned out to be very interesting.

I found out on that retreat that instead of retiring from the money management business, I was about to cash in on some bold new concepts that had been quietly brewing inside of me for the past two years, ever since I had attended evening classes at Regent University's Biblical Studies masters program. One of my courses was "The Life and Teachings of Christ." There in His teachings, guess what I found? Money! We had to write a term paper on Jesus' teachings, so without hesitation I asked if I could write on what Jesus said about money. I had spent my life chasing money, but now that I had some of it, I felt guilty! As a Christian, I began to wonder if it was theologically appropriate for me to be wealthy.

So where did I start? I had the assignment that I wanted, so I turned to the New Testament and began highlighting (with green, of course, the color of money) every reference to money, gold, riches, wealth, and mammon. I restricted my search to the Gospels, the first four books of the New Testament, paying close attention to Jesus' words in red. Then I reduced down those concepts into one page of major themes. What I found was so surprising that I wondered why I had never heard this preached from the pulpit!

1. Ecclesiastes 5:10 NIV.

TWO

JESUS WAS
ALWAYS TALKING
ABOUT MONEY

JESUS SAID I COULD USE MONEY,
BUT I COULDN'T LET IT USE ME.

All my life, I had heard preachers bang their shoe on the pulpit and demand that people tithe. I figured they gave those sermons so that the pastor could feed his kids, because the message always seemed to be delivered with a bit of guilt attached.

But as I dug out of my Bible what Jesus said about money, I found out that money was an important subject to Jesus. He didn't talk much about the Old Testament concept of tithing, but He had more to say about money than any other topic He covered, including heaven and hell. As I continued my study, I discovered three main messages that Jesus gave about money.

JESUS TALKS MONEY

1. Mammon:
   SERVANT OR MASTER?
2. DECEITFULNESS OF RICHES
3. REBUKES AND REWARDS

1. MAMMON: SERVANT OR MASTER?

According to the Old Testament, if I didn't tithe, I was stealing from God.[2] Jesus took it several steps further. He said, "Pick one—only one. You can't serve both God and Money." When I first read Jesus' statement about serving God or Mammon, it seemed simple, almost obvious, but when I thought about it, I realized that many of my decisions had been improperly motivated by money. I asked myself, do my actions and motivations revolve around money, or do I use money as a tool to achieve my goals? Do I use IT, or does IT use me? When I have to make a decision, who decides?

The word for mammon is capitalized in the New Testament. That suggests that for some people Money with a capital *M* is the object of their affections. In other words, it's a god. Money with a small *m* is neutral, while Money with a capital *M* is not.

Serving Money. To be honest, I saw that instead of money serving me, I was serving money. Capital M. What did that mean?

"NO ONE CAN SERVE TWO MASTERS;
FOR EITHER HE WILL HATE THE ONE AND LOVE
THE OTHER, OR ELSE HE WILL BE LOYAL TO
THE ONE AND DESPISE THE OTHER.
YOU CANNOT SERVE GOD AND MAMMON."[3]

It meant that money was dictating my final decisions. I always considered the money factor before I moved forward. I could not serve both God and mammon, Jesus said, and I had to admit I was serving mammon. You don't have to be rich to serve money.

Anything for Money. Some years ago there was a TV show called "Anything for Money." It caught people on the street who were asked to do a variety of silly things for money. When they refused, they were offered more and more money until they finally agreed to do the stunt. I remember watching and thinking how I would respond. What was my price? Yes, I was motivated by money. For example, I thought I should choose a job by which one paid the most, but I was wrong. I was serving money. It ruled me. I could never pay full price for anything. I had to make phone calls at the cheapest rates. I flew only at discounted fares.

When I like or dislike someone who is rich, or feel superior or inferior to them, or treat them differently, it shows that money has power over me. When I asked myself some honest questions, I realized that money can motivate you only if you worship it. Jesus had found me out.

MAKING MONEY MY SERVANT

In my growing understanding of money in the context of servant vs. master, I went through three distinctly separate stages:

First, I was a tightwad. I couldn't spend it or give it away. Not that I had very much, but what little I had, I couldn't bring myself to part with it. When God revealed to me that money was only a tool to be used to accomplish things, I remember well the defining moment when I impulsively crumpled up a five dollar bill and threw it over my shoulder. I was in charge! Money was not going to rule my life. I refused to keep serving it any longer. It was not going to be my master.

WHO'S IN CHARGE, ME OR MONEY?

DID I PICK MY CAREER BASED ON
HOW MUCH IT PAID? *Yes.*

MUST I BUY THINGS ON SALE? *Yes.*

WAS I MOTIVATED BY A FREE TRIP
OR FREE SAMPLE? *Yes.*

DID I EAT MORE FOOD IF SOMEONE ELSE
WAS PAYING FOR IT? *Yes.*

DID I EVER BUY SOMETHING I DIDN'T NEED
WHEN IT WAS ON SALE? *Yes.*

WAS MORE MONEY MY GOAL? *Yes.*

DID I FEAR BEING TAKEN ADVANTAGE
OF FINANCIALLY? *Yes.*

DID I REACT TO REQUESTS FOR MONEY
WITH INDIGNATION OR ANGER? *Yes.*

DID I HAVE TROUBLE SPENDING MONEY
EVEN WHEN I HAD IT? *Yes.*

DID I EVER DEDUCT A PERSONAL ITEM
AS A BUSINESS EXPENSE? *Yes.*

WAS I USING MONEY
OR WAS MONEY USING ME?

In the next stage, when I realized that I was in charge of my money, I was into prosperity thinking. I began to buy anything I wanted. "Money is my slave" became the theme. I would buy items because they were more expensive. Fortunately, this second phase of dealing with money did not last too long and ended with an interesting lunch-time message from God, which led me into the final stage of stewardship.

Finally, stewardship. I was having lunch alone at a sub shop that had a video game in the corner. After I finished my sandwich, I got up in front of the "Centipede," as it was called. As I put in the quarter and heard it get swallowed, I heard a voice inside me that asked the question, "Whose quarter was that?" There was no one standing behind me, so I knew Who was asking me. And I knew the answer right away. It was God's quarter in my pocket—well, now it was in the Centipede.

THE CENTIPEDE INTRODUCED ME TO MY FIRST LESSON ON THE RESPONSIBILITIES OF WEALTH, THAT EVERYTHING BELONGS TO GOD, AND IS TO BE MANAGED BY ME.

As God said to Job, "Everything under the heaven belongs to Me." [4] And David said, "Everything in the heavens and earth is yours, O Lord, and this is your kingdom. We adore you as being in control of everything. Riches and honor come from you alone, and you are the Ruler of all mankind." [5]

2. Deceitfulness Of Riches

In the parable of the sower, Jesus talked about "the deceitfulness of riches."

> *Now he who received seed among the thorns is he who hears the word, and the cares of this world and the deceitfulness of riches choke the word, and he becomes unfruitful.*[6]

How can riches be deceitful, if I'm not careful?

Riches can lure me into a trap. Why did Jesus call money deceitful? It's not what it seems. It's like a fish lure that looks attractive to a fish until he gets it in his mouth. When he finds out, by then it's too late. He's been tricked.

Riches can jeopardize my relationship with God. Jesus said that not only are riches deceitful, but also wealth causes a person to become spiritually unfruitful. This seems to imply that having wealth negates my need for a relationship with God and my dependency on Him, because I form a dependency on money instead. An independent person who does not depend on God will become spiritually bankrupt and not bear fruit as he travels the road of self-indulgence.

Riches can result in greed. No one likes to think of themselves as greedy, but greed is such a sneaky sin that it blinds you in a way that other things do not. To do a quick "greed check," ask yourself how much you dislike seeing greed in others. The more intensely you react to others' greed, the more likely it is that you have an issue with greed yourself. As Jesus said, "Judge not, that you be not judged." [7] Watch out for those areas where you tend to be most judgmental. That may give you some clues to your own weaknesses.

Money doesn't buy happiness. I found from doing estate planning with very wealthy people that they are some of the unhappiest people on the planet. That's because they are fooled by the deceitfulness of their wealth. They think they should hang onto it at all costs.

No matter how much money you have, you always want more. I thought that having more money would satisfy me, but it didn't. That was a deception, too. The money that I had in my hands was giving me that anxiety on Black Monday and every other day.

It's tougher to make sacrifices. The rich young ruler deserted Jesus when He told him what was required for eternal life. Hearing that he should give his possessions to the poor, he sadly walked away. Jesus told His disciples that "it is easier for a camel to go through the eye of a needle than for a rich man to

enter the kingdom of God." [8] This does not say it's impossible, but implies that it would be better not to have riches. And why did He say to give directly to the poor, and not to some worthy self-help organization? My guess? Because they can't repay you.

Happiness is giving

Patrick Morley, author, businessman, president of a charitable organization, has dealt with wealthy businessmen for decades. His insight in a condensed version goes something like this:

> THE GREATER PROPORTION OF A MAN'S INCOME THAT HE GIVES, THE HAPPIER HE IS. HAPPINESS IS NOT WHAT YOU KEEP. THAT'S A DECEPTION. IT'S WHAT YOU GIVE.

3. Rebukes And Rewards

We serve a God Who is just and fair with both His rebukes and His rewards. When we think an injustice has occurred, our understanding is usually limited to our lifetime. God exercises His justice over a much longer time frame—eternity, to be more exact. Jesus talks a great deal about rebukes, as well as rewards, from the perspective of eternity.

Rebuked for foolish hoarding. Jesus teaches without reservation that there is a coming judgment on all those who hoard wealth for themselves. He tells a story about a rich landowner whose harvest yielded more than his storage barns could hold, so he tore down the existing barns and built new and bigger ones. Instead of giving away the surplus, he hoarded it.

> *Then he said, "Here's what I'll do: I'll tear down my barns and build bigger ones. Then I'll gather in all my grain and goods, and I'll say to myself, 'Self, you've done well! You've got it made and can now retire. Take it easy and have the time of your life!' "*
>
> *Just then God showed up and said, "Fool! Tonight you die. And your barnful of goods—who gets it?"*
>
> *That's what happens when you fill your barn with Self and not with God.*[9]

This affluent person's life was selfish and superficial. He went from affluence to luxury. He did not stop to think that perhaps the reason God made him affluent was so he could pass something on to the less fortunate. A businessman might call him

prudent. God called him a fool and will judge him on his actions.

Suffering for insensitivity. Another story Jesus told was about a rich man who dressed well and feasted every night.[10] Outside his house a beggar named Lazarus lay in the road. He was diseased and crippled, and all he wanted was some of the crumbs from the rich man's feast. The two men died the same day and the rich man found himself tormented in hell. Lazarus was at peace in heaven. The rich man now begged for a drop of water from Lazarus, but there was a gulf separating heaven and hell, and the rich man must live for eternity in torment—irrevocable judgment based on his own actions on earth.

Using Mammon unrighteously. Jesus said that "the children of this world are in their generation wiser than the children of light."[11] Then He said, "And I tell you, make friends for yourselves by means of unrighteous mammon, so that when it fails they may receive you into the eternal habitations."[12] When Jesus spoke of "unrighteous mammon" He was underscoring the inherent "fallenness" of money when it is misused. Unrighteousness is a necessary attribute of the god of Mammon. It is issued and enforced under the authority of a man-made government. By putting the descriptive adjective "unrighteous" on mammon, Jesus prevents us from ever taking a naive view of wealth.

Preparation for the future with something other than money. Jesus is telling us to use money in such a way that when it fails—and it will fail—we have prepared for our future.

Poisoned by loving money. The love of money is poison and the power of money is virtually unlimited. Money can buy people or eliminate people. It can buy prestige, honor or allegiance, even when they are not deserved.

REWARDS

Right use of money has two effects:
• It provides rewards of an eternal nature.
• It draws our affections into the kingdom of God.

> "FOR WHERE YOUR TREASURE IS,
> THERE WILL YOUR HEART BE ALSO."[13]

Here are some examples of how money can be used for righteous purposes that God says are worthy of reward:

Using money to make friends for the future. In Luke 16, Jesus tells a parable quite different from all the others mentioned in the Gospels. A wealthy man discovers that his business manager has been mishandling

his funds and promptly fires him, but before his termination becomes final, the steward devises a plan to insure his future. He contacts his employer's creditors and writes off 20 to 50 percent of their debts. These people are now indebted to him. Later, when he is out of a job, they will be obligated to help him.

Even though what the business manager had done may have been dishonest, when the master found out he was so impressed with the manager's cleverness that he commended him. Jesus is not teaching dishonesty here, but illustrating an important spiritual truth. He highlights the manager's shrewdness in using economic resources for non-economic goals—using money to make friends for a later time.

MAKING FRIENDS BY MEANS OF "UNRIGHTEOUS MAMMON" MEANS THAT WE ARE TO TAKE IT AND USE IT FOR GOD'S PURPOSES. WE MUST NOT BE OVERCOME BY ITS EVIL BIAS, BUT RATHER THAN REJECT IT WE SHOULD CONQUER IT AND USE IT FOR ADVANCING THE KINGDOM OF GOD.

Using money to get things done. Money can accomplish things on God's agenda and put citizens to work on behalf of advancing the kingdom of God.

Stockpiling treasures in the next world. This is the "greater use" that Jesus refers to. He warns against building treasures on earth that are insecure and corrupt. He says, "Don't hoard treasure down here where it gets eaten by moths and corroded by rust or—worse!—stolen by burglars. Stockpile treasure in heaven, where it's safe from moth and rust and burglars." [14]

Using money for God's purposes. It seems that this greater use is the only justification for being a wealthy Christian. Those called to this ministry had better be obedient to God's calling in this area. It is a dangerous place to be—like being behind enemy lines during a war. Richard Foster called the money ministry of a Christian "living close to hell for the sake of heaven."

> *This path is fraught with great frustrations and temptations, and those who walk it have to face perplexing decisions and tragic moral choices that most people will never have to consider.*
>
> *In many ways our life will be immensely more complex, though it does not need to be complicated. We will need the prayer and support of the people of God who must stand by us, counsel us, guide us. We will be living close to hell for the sake of heaven.* [15]

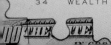

Receiving rewards or "paychecks" in heaven. Jesus said that He rewards those whose work fulfills His purposes. The concept of a reward in heaven is illustrated in New Testament teaching by the use of the Greek word in Matthew 16:27 that is translated as "reward," which literally means "paycheck." This eternal compensation is not a gift, but an actual payback or settlement of a debt commensurate with the action that was done on His behalf, in His name, by His people. Jesus says that when He returns, "the Son of Man is going to come in His Father's glory with His angels, and then He will reward (paycheck) each person according to what he's done."[16]   In the last verses in the Bible, He says, "Behold, I am coming soon! My reward (paycheck) is with me, and I'll give to everyone according to what he has done."[17] Or as it says in The Message, "Yes, I'm on my way! I'll be there soon! I'm bringing my payroll with me. I'll pay all people in full for their life's work."[18]

Increasing my permanent net worth. I have an account in heaven where my permanent net worth is being increased by my giving here on earth. Whatever money I accumulate on earth is temporary net worth, but there is something greater going on in my behalf in the next world—something permanent.

Why didn't I hear about this concept of permanent wealth earlier in my life? Did no one ever tell me, or did

I just choose not to listen because I had a different agenda? Now that I knew this information, what was I going to do with it? Why bother working? I should just quit and retire, since my selfish ambition of chasing money seemed to be a dead end street. That's when I walked into the biggest deal of my life.

2. Malachi 3:9.

3. Matthew 6:24. Capitalized according to original text.

4. Job 41:11.

5. I Chronicles 29: 11-12 TLB.

6. Matthew 13:22 NKJV.

7. Matthew 7:1 NKJV.

8. Luke 18:24-25 NIV.

9. Luke 12:18-21 The Message.

10.Luke 16:19-31.

11. Luke 16:8 KJV.

12.Luke16:9 RSV.

13. Matthew 6:21 KJV.

14. Matthew 6:19-20 The Message.

15. Richard Foster, *Freedom of Simplicity*, (Harper Collins, 1982), p. 129.

16. Matthew 16:27 NIV.

17. Revelation 22:12.

18. Revelation 22:12 *The Message*.

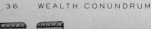

THREE

THE DEAL

GOD OWNS IT ALL, BUT HE
GIVES ME THE RESPONSIBILITY OF
MANAGING IT FOR HIM.

Climbing up a trail at sunrise in the mountains of West Virginia, it was a bit nippy that October morning. My emotions were still raw after the recent near miss on Black Monday. I had gone on a retreat to try to hear from God about my plans to retire from the money management business. The seeds of Jesus' teachings on money had been germinating inside of me ever since I had written that term paper two years earlier about whether or not Christians should have wealth.

Even though I was only 40, I was ready to retire from all that stress. I talked to several retired folks at the retreat about their retirement and how they were able to get out of the frantic business world and have some fun. I told them that I was an investment advisor and estate planner who was going to quit and see what retirement was like. This was my lifelong dream—retirement, financial independence, and security. But why did that seem so self-serving and empty to me now? That was why I was climbing that trail to hear from God.

It's hard for me to listen for God's voice when I'm in a tight spot. Usually I do the talking. However, this turned out to be one of those times when I heard God and I knew that He heard me. I had a dialogue with God that woke me up to a new way of looking at my life, the way I handled money, and my relationship with Him.

God does not speak to me audibly, but He speaks in a Still, Small, Voice that is so loud it hits me like a 2x4. I know with absolute certainty that I have heard His voice, even if I can't explain it to anyone else.

God is whispering truth to me a whole lot more than I am listening for it, but I am either not interested or I am tuned out because I am busy going over Niagara Falls in a barrel every day. My best listening times come when I first wake up in the morning, or at a church

worship service, or at a retreat where I can get quiet for several days of abstaining from my daily activities.

On this retreat, I was about to have a dialogue with God and make a deal that changed my whole perspective on this money business.

DIALOGUE WITH GOD

"Good morning, Lord. What a spectacular sunrise!"

"I made it just for you to enjoy."

"You are pretty cool. I acknowledge and worship You for Your creative genius."

" I love you."

"Why? I haven't really done anything worthwhile."

"I know, I love you no matter what you do."

"Why?"

"It is Who I Am."

"Well, I am struggling with my life."

"I know."

"Can You help?"

"You were not made to handle money the way you do. It will destroy you."

"I know. I certainly can't invest for clients and enjoy my life."

"Why do you say that?"

"Because the market churns me up so much that my life becomes too painful. I get upset and depressed and the result is that all my relationships suffer—wife, kids, employees—and I become an emotional basket case."

"I have noticed. It makes Me sad."

"Well, it won't happen any more. I will do something else with my life."

"So you are running from the problem?"

"What other options do I have? I hate every day."

"Do you really want to know?"

"YES! HELP!"

"Whose money are you investing?"

"Mine."

"YOURS?"

" Well, I suppose it is actually Yours."

" And who owns the business you run?"

"I do."

"YOU do?"

"Well, the money I invest is Yours, but the business is mine."

"You need to rethink that."

"What do You mean?"

"When you own the business, all the responsibilities and stress fall on you, and I did not make you to withstand all those pressures."

"You mean all these years I thought I was in charge and tried to get You to work for me?"

"Yes, you asked Me to bless you and make you rich. But you weren't built to handle all those responsibilities. And you weren't built to handle all the profits, either."

"I am beginning to see what You are saying. Instead of You working for me, I should work for You? It will be Your business?"

"Yes, but you don't get the profits. They are Mine."

"Let me get this straight, You get the profits? What do You want with them?"

"There are lots of very important things that I would like to do, but the people who want to accomplish them do not have the funds. Even as we speak now, they are in tears petitioning Me for funds to do very urgent and necessary things."

"So You want my profits to be given to them?"

" No, I want MY profits to be given to them."

"I am beginning to see . . . but if I do this business venture, how am I supposed to deal with the stress, which is why I quit?"

"I will take it from you. Since it is no longer YOUR business, you will find peace."

"O.K., Lord, You're the Boss, but if I have these problems again, I will quit and do something else."

"Agreed."

"You have a deal!"

THE DEAL WITH GOD

The difference between a deal with the devil and a deal with God is that the devil is a taker and God is a Giver. I had no idea where we were going from here, but I was willing. In the *Chronicles of Narnia* by C.S. Lewis, a child named Lucy nervously asks Mr. Beaver about

Aslan, the lion in the story who symbolically represents Jesus, and she gets this response:

> "Then he isn't safe?" said Lucy.
> "Safe?" said Mr. Beaver; "don't you hear what Mrs. Beaver tells you? Who said anything about safe? 'Course he isn't safe. But he's good. He's the King, I tell you."[19]

For those who think working a deal with God is mundane, boring, predictable and safe, you don't know the God Whom I was learning to deal with. Over the years, I had read a lot of deals in *Forbes Magazine* looking for my own rainbow and pot of gold to appear. No one warned me to put on my seat belt for this ride, but I should have! I was about to walk into a business deal better than any I had ever read about in *Forbes*.

19. C. S. Lewis, *The Lion, the Witch and the Wardrobe* (New York: HarperCollins Publishers, 1978), p. 81.

FOUR

MAKING MEGABUCKS

With God as the Owner,
the cash flowed.

My method of trading funds at the time of the market crash of October 1987 had protected myself and my small group of private investors from catastrophic losses. My dialogue with God on the retreat in West Virginia shortly afterwards had given me something else—the knowledge that it was no longer me carrying the load alone. God was with me.

I was no longer alone.
God was with me.

My advisory company was called Spectrum Financial, Inc., possibly related to the pot of gold at the end of the rainbow. I had been able to develop several trading strategies so that whenever the stock market became technically unhealthy, I was able to sell out of the mutual funds into the safety of a money market.

Spectrum Financial functioned as a fee-based advisor rather than as a stockbroker. Our income was tied to their increase. We had no incentive for trading other than maximizing client investment returns and lowering risk. Instead of making profits from clients' accounts by trading stocks on commission, we made money from the growth of the assets that we managed for our clients.

Maximizing Profits

It seemed that investing was something that I did well. How did I define "well"? Making lots of money in up markets and not losing much in down markets.

OUR INITIAL STRATEGY INVOLVED THREE CONCEPTS.

1. Trading mutual funds
2. Compound interest
3. Preservation of principal and limiting losses

1. *Trading mutual funds.* Mutual funds, at the time we began, seemed to be the best vehicle for investing that I had seen anywhere. Mutual funds had it all—diversification, management, and minimal charges to exchange stock and bond funds quickly into the safety of a cash position.

2. *Compound interest* was the greatest wealth builder I had ever found. An 18 percent annual return will nearly double your money every four years. One dollar becomes two becomes four becomes eight over a 12-year period. At 25 percent interest, one dollar

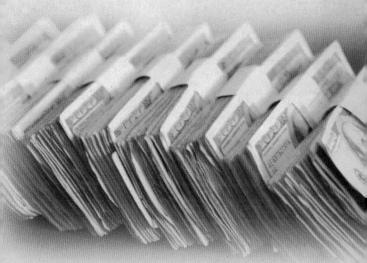

becomes $14.55 in 12 years. That is the power of compound interest. I had discovered this financial principle and was committed to applying it to amass wealth for both myself and my clients.

3. *Preservation of principal and limiting losses.* Preservation of principal was a key to investment success. Loss of principal was tremendously costly. For example, a 50 percent loss on an account would require a 100 percent gain just to get back to even again.

It is easy to talk about limiting losses. It is harder to actually do it all the time. Two major items cause a stock trader to perform poorly. One is the fear and greed syndrome, the other is ego (otherwise known as pride). I seemed to have gotten past the fear (afraid to lose it), and greed (want to make lots of it fast). But the pride issues in my life are still being negotiated.

BARRON'S INVESTMENT CONTEST

During the first several years of operation, Spectrum Financial entered an investment contest sponsored by a national consulting firm that verified investment performance of various money managers and reported the numbers. In October 1991 Barron's financial magazine published several articles about the performance of Spectrum in this contest because it was so remarkable. When I was interviewed by Barron's,

I spoke openly about Who owned the business (God) and how prayer was important to the investment decisions of the firm. As a result of these articles, our phone rang off the hook, and we continued to grow at an amazing rate.

One new client flew in from New York
to meet with our staff.
As I was driving him to the airport,
he asked me if I really prayed
about investment decisions. We had a
good discussion about this new concept
of business ownership by God!

Business Referrals From Friends

During this time I was involved with a business study group of about ten members from all over the country who focused on estate planning for wealthy clients. We would meet once a year at a resort to discuss business as well as personal issues. Each member made a presentation to the other members of the group and talked about the most effective and profitable ideas of the preceding year. We still meet annually after 25 years, and lifetime bonds have resulted from these relationships, not to mention the business opportunities we have discovered and shared.

A BUSINESS STUDY GROUP IS
ONE OF THE BEST SOURCES OF ACQUIRING
PRACTICAL BUSINESS IDEAS
THAT I COULD RECOMMEND TO ANYONE.

At the request of several members of the study group, I began to manage investments for their clients. With the market crash of 1987 still fresh in the minds of investors and the bull market of the 1990s reinforcing the need for safe yet profitable investments, business began to pour in.

Our business prospered. The growth was amazing! I saw assets under management double every nine months. I remember always having stacks of new account contracts requiring my signature.

I wasn't upset about the market the way I had been before. Well, maybe a little anxiety remained, but not the sleepless-night kind. I sometimes had a little uneasiness with trading, but this time it was due to ego problems, not loss of money. More about that later.

ADVISOR TO OTHER INVESTMENT FIRMS

As the firm grew, it became larger than I could manage effectively. The size of our investment assets was beginning to limit the performance of some of our investment programs.

I felt that I needed to get smaller to become more effective, so I arranged for some of the larger accounts to be split off into separate, newly formed advisory firms where they purchased our advice for their clients. I made an arrangement to sell investment recommendations to other fee-based advisors for their clients.

And still we grew quickly! I eventually developed several systems to conform to the limitations of new legislation related to mutual fund trading.

We developed our own concept of using several hedge fund strategies within mutual funds that we designed. We can now invest in new and better ways to limit risk and maximize returns, sometimes being very aggressive, and sometimes being totally in a cash position. And now there are no longer any limitations on the amount of assets we can effectively manage.

We invest today for a broad scope of clients—from little old ladies with nest eggs to corporations with retirement plans and endowment funds.

TAKING THE RISK OF TRUSTING GOD

In my younger years when I sought God for direction, I was led to this Scripture in Proverbs:

> *Trust God from the bottom of your heart;*
> *Don't try to figure out everything on your own.*

Listen for God's voice in everything you do,
everywhere you go;
he's the one who will keep you on track.[20]

That verse unsettled me at first. What would happen if I gave God everything with no restrictions? No limits? It was a tough decision, but I said yes, and asked God for faith to allow whatever would happen next.

How did God want me to spend these megabucks? What did He want me to give to others? My charitable giving was picking up speed, but it was a slow process of walking out my faith. I still had sticky fingers. I had a long way to go.

DON'T EVER TURN YOUR LIFE OVER TO GOD AND EXPECT THE ORDINARY!

STUNNED BY GANDHI'S LIFE

I had an opportunity to see the movie *Gandhi*, a story about the leader who was responsible for bringing independence to India. The movie had a profound impact on me. Here was a simple man who gave his life to liberate his people from unspeakable poverty and unjust government rule. He did it by living like an ordinary citizen, and preaching and demonstrating a message of nonviolence.

At the end of the movie I was stunned. The contrast between his life and mine was put before me in a magnitude so huge it depressed me. I usually like movies that make me feel good at the end. This one made me feel down—about myself, my life, my accomplishments, my selfish ambition. Somehow way down inside I had a desire to make a difference, too. But I didn't know how or where to start. I felt like a total failure.

It was time for another dialogue with God.

DIALOGUE WITH GOD

"I am depressed."

"How can I help? I Am (here for you)."

"I feel so worthless, and selfish."

"I love you."

"How can You love me when I am so selfish?"

"It is Who I Am."

"How can I do something worthwhile? I don't have anything that I am good at."

"You have your will, and you have Me at your side. What is it that you want?"

"I want to make a difference in this world, but I don't know how to start."

"You just started something of great significance."

"How?"

"You asked for My help."

"Why is that significant?"

"Because you asked for help and confessed that you couldn't do it alone."

"You mean a partnership?"

"Yes, but different than you expect. You are not responsible for doing the changing. You are responsible for confessing your failures, and that releases Me to make the changes in your life."

"So my job is to recognize my shortcomings and ask for help?"

"Yes."

"That seems so simple. There must be more to it."

"Yes, there is one more critical element."

"What is that?"

"Faith—you must let go and BELIEVE that I will change things."

"How does this all work? I have to understand to have faith."

"Faith does not require understanding. If it did, it would not be faith. Does a farmer plant seed in the field and understand? He just understands that it grows if it has the proper environment. Plant your seed by confessing your sin to Me, and nourish it by believing that I will create in your heart a new life, filled with My purposes."

"It seems so simple, and yet so difficult."

"It is both."

"I really don't deserve it."

"You don't, but that is what My Grace is all about—unmerited favor."

"Then all I can do is thank You."

At that time I had no idea where I was headed with my future giving, how many lives would be affected, and how my level of giving would somehow turn around and make me even wealthier. I had to go through a humbling experience that broke my pride as I saw "the poorest of the poor" and the extraordinary woman who ministered to them. I still didn't understand how serious God had been when He told me about those in tears who were petitioning Him for funds for their very urgent and necessary needs. I was about to find out.

20. Proverbs 3:5-6 *The Message.*

FIVE

CONFRONTATION IN CALCUTTA

I LEARNED SOMETHING
UNCOMFORTABLE ABOUT MYSELF AND
MONEY WHEN I WAS CONFRONTED
WITH THE TRULY NEEDY.

For some time I had been wrestling with the fact that my finances had gotten out of control, that money had me in its grip. I wanted to be a better servant, a better father, a better husband, a better friend. Money was always on my mind.

I was reading a great deal about money and my relationship with it, and somehow I got on a mailing list for an organization called The Ministry of Money. Strange name. Stranger message.

It seemed that they had an organization that existed solely for the purpose of helping people like me who loved money too much—like an Alcoholics Anonymous for the rich—to help wealthy people deal with the issues of wealth addiction.

THE "SEVEN YEAR TURN"

At one of their seminars they said that once you see the money problem in your life and begin to deal with it, it can take at least seven years to work it out. Instead of being down on myself, I allowed myself time to begin to resolve the money issues in my life. Like pushing the tiller on a huge ship, I began what I called the "Seven Year Turn." It was the beginning of a new chapter of self-denial and self-discovery.

Involvement with this group included not only a weekend seminar but also other exercises like the writing of an autobiography that covered the money issues in my life.

LEARNING ABOUT LOVE FROM MOTHER TERESA

Then came the big step. A "hands on" assignment of what they call a "trip of reverse mission." This involved going to the streets of Calcutta, India, to work with Mother Teresa and the Sisters of Charity, ministering to the poorest of the poor at Kalighat, a home for the destitute and dying. The trip began to work in me long before I reached our destination, so I wrote about it in my journal:

> God, help me learn about love from Mother Teresa—burn it into my heart. Make my changes permanent. Make them large, make them quick. Push me to my limit, God. I'm dissatisfied with my past slow progress. Your ways are always new. Teach me Your ways.

SCENES OF SQUALOR

As we landed at the airport, deformed children and beggars ran up to us. Then we drove in silent disbelief, seeing the squalor. In my journal I struggled to adequately describe the experience:

> All the people—dirty, mutilated, and humble—busy at their tasks of survival. From the safety of the taxi, my eyes met the eyes of women and children; I could not allow myself to look for long, as my eyes dropped from theirs. Something in their eyes made me feel embarrassed, almost guilty. The differences between us—my wealth and

their poverty—are so extreme. I may have more than one million of them put together. Is that fair?

I close my eyes and see thousands of people scurrying about, cows, goats, and deformed dogs roaming the streets, women with babies begging for milk money, children defecating on the curb and begging, too; barefoot rickshaw drivers, people bathing at street side. What do I say to the children begging me for money?

Why do the beggars annoy me so? They just smile and keep asking. I was about to buy a piece of chocolate at the corner shop, but a woman beggar chased me away. I couldn't "pig out" on chocolate when she probably didn't have dinner tonight.

Each one of us on the team was affected differently by our day's activities. We met daily for sharing and discussion. Each of us was getting exposed to life in a way that we could not deny or walk away from as many travelers do when they visit poverty-infested places. Each of us shared our own issues and revelation.

Reality continued to assault our senses as we worked. We washed clothes, bathed

the ill, handed out food and medicine, and did physical therapy for these terminally ill patients.

I watched people die. This was not TV.

I walked across the street with a friend to a community dump that smelled so bad I wanted to vomit. Little children picked through the garbage, looking for plastic bags or bottles that may have some value. I breathed through my mouth as I watched them—but the smell didn't seem to bother them. They lived in the dump, in makeshift cardboard structures. I thought about my own home, how big it was: one month's electric bill was more than these people made in a lifetime.

PRIVATE MEETING WITH MOTHER

Shortly after our arrival, we had a private meeting with Mother Teresa—a short, frail woman with a beautiful smile and bare, gnarled feet. "Pray for our sisters and their work," was her greeting. The 400 sister houses founded by this remarkable woman are dedicated to alleviating the suffering of the most destitute families all over the world. She loves them all dearly. I wrote in my journal:

She had a singleness of purpose that was intense, but she was incredibly low-key and light hearted.

She told stories—one was about a beggar who wanted to give all he collected that day to Mother's work. She knew that to take it he would go hungry, and to not receive it would be unfair to him. As she received his gift, she saw the joy on his face. She also told of a five-year-old girl who

*gave her entire allowance with a note which
said, "I love you, Mother Teresa."*

    *She is an amazing person; I am learning
much from her. As I listened to her speak,
my eyes filled with tears.*

    *We went to the leper colony today. I was
touched by the joy in their smiles and the
pride in their work. A group of blind lepers
sang a worship song in their native tongue
while we were there. Translated, it said,
"Jesus be my eyes, be my legs." I was aware
that it was Thanksgiving Day and I was
more conscious about being thankful than
on any other Thanksgiving Day.*

I wished that my children could understand what
was going on while they were home watching TV,
drinking Cokes, and complaining that their turkey
was overcooked, or that someone had forgotten the
whipped cream for the pumpkin pie.

You can't go home the same person when you
take a mission trip like this. Something snapped inside
of me on that trip. I wasn't so demanding. I wasn't so
fussy. I was much more grateful about just about
everything. I didn't get upset about small things the

way I had before. I didn't need as much stuff. I had a
new desire to give.

> How much I need Jesus to change me!
> I am without strength. But I feel as though
> I'm having a major victory over "self" and a
> major death is taking place within me.
> Praise God! God, change me—go deep
> within, yank out the ugly root of self and
> help me to stop just toying with it. Remove
> it and fill the void with Jesus and His love.
> Help me to stop trying to be "Christian"
> from the outside in, but change me within
> so Your works flow out of me.

COMMUNION AND GOD'S GRACE

When Mother Teresa served communion to us in
Calcutta, I saw the love and grace of God in her eyes.
As I knelt down, I became aware of my sinful nature,
and repeated the phrase to myself, "Lord, have mercy
on a sinner such as me."

A sin is anything I do that takes me in a direction
away from God. God brings sins to my mind if I ask
Him, but makes me responsible for confession of my
sins. That means calling a spade a spade, no beating
around the bush, accepting the fact that my behavior

and attitude are wrong—again. It means repenting, changing my attitude, being sorry, and asking God to change me from the inside out.

I had always taken pride in trying to change myself, and when I failed, I felt guilty. That is like walking through a marsh and feeling guilty because my feet are muddy. I try to keep out of the marsh, but let's face it, I'm going to get in there from time to time.

GOING TO COMMUNION IS LIKE
ASKING JESUS TO CLEAN YOUR SHOES
BECAUSE YOU HAVE NO ARMS
TO CLEAN THEM YOURSELF. I WANT TO CLEAN
THEM MYSELF! I DON'T WANT ANY HELP.

I used to be afraid of going to church to celebrate communion on the first Sunday of the month. It was a time of introspection and dredging up all the things I did wrong since my last communion. Of course, I knew I was not supposed to wait the entire month before confessing sin, but that often was the case with me. I would avoid examining my life like avoiding my annual prostate exam. I never understood this transaction. I sinned, I was sorry. O.K., but the next time the same sin popped up again. So am I supposed to confess again? I promised that I wouldn't last time, and now I am here again. I began to always feel guilty and hated communion.

PARTNERSHIP WITH GOD

After reading a book by Watchman Nee entitled *The Normal Christian Life* I finally got the big picture. Partnership! I can't do what God does, and He won't do what I need to do. The inner change of my heart is a work of grace. Just as the tiny germinating mustard seed grows into a large tree, my very nature changes into His Image. I love communion now. When I see the communion table set up in front as I enter a church, I choke up a bit and give thanks as I ask for assistance with my sinful state. When my pride issues come back to life, I just confess them.

> I CAN'T CHANGE MY OWN NATURE, ONLY GOD CAN. CONFESSION AND FAITH ARE MY PART, THEN GOD BEGINS CHANGING MY ATTITUDES, BEHAVIORS, AND IMPROPER THOUGHTS FROM THE INSIDE OUT.

Amazing grace! How sweet the sound
That saved a wretch like me!
I once was lost, but now am found;
Was blind, but now I see.

I was humbled, forgiven, in partnership with God,
and being prepared for a faster pace.

SIX

EMPTYING THE BARNS

I COULDN'T CHALLENGE OTHERS TO
EMPTY THEIR WALLETS WHEN I HAD A
BARN STUFFED FULL OF CASH.

Mother Teresa had said, "Anything that is not given is lost." As I was talking about giving to a group of major donors to a Christian ministry, I mentioned her eternal perspective on how God looks at our giving. I thought this ministry did a great job of evangelizing people with the Gospel, so I said, "What you do with your donations is so significant that if you really understood the effectiveness of each dollar, you would not leave the room with any cash in your wallet."

Now here I was preaching to myself. I still had millions in my foundation and I was telling people to empty their wallets.

When I had lunch with one of the board members we had a discussion about the size of the "barn" where I kept my funds for giving. I said to him, "If I really believe what I'm saying, I will actually do something about emptying my barn."

GIVING AWAY FIFTY PERCENT

When I started pulling down big bucks, I wanted to make sure that as a steward of God's assets, I gave responsibly. Looking at current income tax law, I realized that I could deduct up to 50 percent of my adjusted gross income each year for charitable giving. If I gave less than 50 percent, I lost the allowable deduction forever. I could not make it up the next year. Since my income went up so quickly, sometimes I had to scramble to make certain that I gave at least 50 percent by the end of the year. At the end of one year I got caught with more money than I knew what to do with, so I quickly called my lawyer and set up a private foundation to invest the funds for future gifts. I stuffed it full of cash.

I called this "warehousing funds" for future charitable giving. It sounded like a good idea at the time.

Tax law required me to distribute from the foundation a minimum of five percent of the investments (gains) each year, but anything over and above that would grow neatly into a big pile of cash. Thanks to compound interest, the money was growing tax-free in a foundation account that would become a giant wad of money, as my IRA had done. Maybe some day I would take the time to give it away, or let my children give it away after I was gone. Meanwhile, I could sit on it and watch it grow and feel good about controlling it, even though it was not technically mine.

> INSTEAD OF COMMENDING THE FARMER WHO BUILT BIGGER BARNS, JESUS CALLED HIM A FOOL. I APPLIED THAT ANALOGY TO MYSELF AND MY GROWING FOUNDATION.

As I mentioned in Chapter 2, Jesus told about a wealthy farmer who had such a great harvest that he didn't have enough room to store it all. He decided to tear down his small barns and build bigger ones to hold all his prosperity.

I had millions of dollars in my foundation. I had been trading them so excessively that I had to move the money to another financial institution just because the fund was growing so large.

Moving The Seed Out Of The Barns

Over the next several months I thought and prayed about what to do about this injustice of too much money in my barns.

The money I keep in my foundation is like apple seeds stored in a barn. My objective is to get the largest apple harvest that I can. If I trickle out the seeds at five percent a year, how many apple trees will get planted? Not many.

Seeds reproduce much faster when they are planted and allowed to grow than if they stay in the barn until some future planting date. Seeds left in the barn can lose their value. They may be eaten by insects. They may be destroyed by rain or fire damage, like a stock market crash.

JOHNNY APPLESEED

One young man who knew the value of planting seeds instead of keeping them in the barn was Johnny Appleseed (John Chapman). Beginning in 1800, when he was 26 years old, and continuing for the next 50 years,

HE TOOK HIS APPLE SEEDS WEST.
HE TRAVELED AHEAD OF THE PIONEERS,
PREPARING THE WAY WITH APPLE TREES THAT
HE HAD PLANTED. MANY TOWNS
WERE FOUNDED LATER NEAR THE SITES OF
THE JOHNNY APPLESEED TREE NURSERIES.

I like the story of Johnny Appleseed because he is an example of someone who took seeds where they could be used best. He walked the countryside with them, planting apple trees all across America.

I came up with a plan of action that would have an impact in several ways.

PLAN OF ACTION
FOR EMPTYING MY BARNS

1. MATCHING GIFTS OF PRINCIPAL
2. PAYING ALL THE GAINS EVERY YEAR
3. LIMITING THE NUMBER OF BEQUESTS
4. INVESTING WITH GOD FOR GREATER RETURNS
5. BEING AWARE OF THE NEEDS OF OTHERS

1. Matching gifts of principal. First, I decided if I was going to give away what was in my barn, then I would take others down with me. So I initiated a matching gift program with several charitable organizations that I felt were doing the most effective work, and approached them with a plan to get their donors thinking bigger than in the past. I would match dollar for dollar any gifts made not from donors' *income*, but from their *principal*.

This was a new concept for people who used the tithe for their giving standard—10 percent of their *income*. My matching gift program involved sacrificial giving of *principal*. It had the effect of getting people to think bigger, becoming more generous, more creative.

"Do we have property we do not need?"

"Is my retirement plan available for God to use now?"

IT'S NOT THAT DRIBBLING OUT THE PROFITS
FROM A FOUNDATION IS A WRONG THING
TO DO, BUT IT IS SO INFERIOR
TO THE BIG PICTURE OF CURRENT NEEDS,
THAT IT IS FOOLISH.

"Would Jesus have set up a charitable foundation?"

It is interesting to note that those who matched my gift of principal did so right after the stock market top in 2000, after which the NASDAQ proceeded to

fall 70 percent. Not quite so fortunate was a successful businessman by the name of Mike Kendrick, who lost it all in the bear market of 2000-2003. However, he is glad that he at least tithed his income.

Here is what he said at an annual Generous Giving conference about investing in charitable giving while you can:[21]

> *Invest aggressively when you can. How I wish I could get my hands back on that $100 million portfolio that is now gone. Luckily we invested part of that, but what if we had invested all of it? How big would that be in heaven when we get there? We never know how long God is going to let us hold onto the resources. If we sit in fear and hold on, God may say, "You have held it long enough. I am going to give it to somebody who won't hold on to it." So seize that opportunity, because God is going to continue to bless those who live with an open hand.*

I will never forget a woman who contacted me to thank me for encouraging her to give away her savings account for her children's education fund, to sponsor the translation of the Gospel of Luke for the children of Africa. She said the matching gift allowed her to pay for the entire translation. She said with a laugh, "God will provide for my own children when they need it if I give my funds to Him today." She knew the same God I was learning about.

2. Paying ALL the gains every year. I decided to make a big concession, and instead of compounding the money and dribbling out the five percent required by law, I made myself accountable to my foundation board to pay out ALL the gains every year, which we did for several years. That way, I figured that the god of compound interest wouldn't corrupt my foundation, and I wouldn't be prideful of the investment gains and how I was able to grow it into a big pile of assets.

3. Limiting my bequests. When the Israelites received the daily manna to meet their needs, they were instructed not to save for the future, because God would provide for them. My career in estate planning focused on getting the most money to the heirs with as little taxation as possible, but I have come full circle on this topic. My objective now is how to give away as much as possible, yet still provide an education for my children and a modest inheritance for them. If I leave them enough to live on without working, I will steal their opportunity to develop a relationship with God as their provider, and possibly

get them involved in something for which their life was not designed. Passing money to future generations in foundations or generation-skipping trusts makes it unavailable for solving society's current needs.

God has provided society's current wealth to accomplish all that needs to be done in *this* generation. Our challenge is to see the money He has entrusted to us not as our own but as His, to be used for all of His purposes, right now. Let's get our apple trees planted

now so that they will bear fruit for our generation, while we are still here to see it do some good.

DON'T SAVE MANNA UNTIL TOMORROW

EXODUS 16:14,15,19 NIV

WHEN THE DEW WAS GONE, THIN FLAKES
LIKE FROST ON THE GROUND APPEARED ON
THE DESERT FLOOR. WHEN THE
ISRAELITES SAW IT, THEY SAID TO EACH
OTHER, "WHAT IS IT?" FOR THEY DID
NOT KNOW WHAT IT WAS. MOSES SAID TO
THEM, "IT IS THE BREAD THE LORD HAS GIVEN
YOU TO EAT." . . . THEN MOSES SAID
TO THEM, "NO ONE IS TO KEEP
ANY OF IT UNTIL MORNING."
IF THEY DID, IT TURNED ROTTEN.

4. *Investing with God for greater returns.* But I still had a very big pile of assets, and my barn was very full. I began to realize that by keeping assets in my foundation I was keeping God's money out of His reach and within my own reach, even though it seemed like a reasonable response at the time. I needed to be reminded that God's returns are 30-, 60- and 100-fold.

And that means a 10,000 percent return, not the puny 25 percent returns that doubled money every 3 years.

5. *Being aware of the needs of others.* After I returned home from Calcutta, I thought I would feel guilty about the money I had, but that was never the case. I was able to spend money, but had a new awareness of the needs of others. I also had an increased awareness of how much money I still had, and how meaningless it was to continue to amass wealth. I became aware

that even the poorest people in the United States still have some measure of wealth. They are not even aware of it unless they experience the conditions of the poorest of the poor.

In our country we have the ability to at least find a job, a welfare system, and health care. The people I saw in Calcutta would make a great living picking through our garbage.

That is one reason why I made the decision to give the majority of the funds I donate to Third World countries. I also became empathetic toward the position of outsourcing work to the Third World. Yes, it takes certain jobs away from U.S. citizens, but it provides more efficient labor costs and reduced prices for U.S. consumers, while helping to enhance the standard of living in countries where poverty is so prevalent. From God's viewpoint, He sees people, not geographic and political borders.

A Christmas Puzzle

One of my favorite gifts one Christmas was a unique package from my wife, who understands and shares with me the concept of joyful giving.

That year my wife gave me a cardboard barn, stuffed with several surprise gifts she had given anonymously to people and organizations without telling me, which helped us to reduce our net worth and do something good for others. She said it was lots of fun, especially trying to explain to someone involved in arranging these anonymous gifts how her giving was a gift to me.

It was puzzling to them—a wealth conundrum most people couldn't understand. How could it possibly work for someone to make money and then give it all away? What kind of a business was I running, anyway?

21. Source: http://www.generousgiving.org.

THE WEALTH CONUNDRUM

EARNING MONEY TO MAKE A PROFIT
SO THAT YOU CAN GIVE IT AWAY
IS A CONUNDRUM—BUT IT
REWARDS WELL. "FOR WHOEVER
WANTS TO SAVE HIS LIFE WILL LOSE
IT, BUT WHOEVER LOSES HIS LIFE
FOR ME WILL FIND IT." —JESUS

I run an investment advisory business to make money, then I give away as much of that money as possible to people and organizations who will make a significant difference somewhere. These two types of actions—making it, then giving it away—may seem at first glance to be the opposite of one another, but upon closer examination they are quite similar. It is a paradox. A mystery. A wealth conundrum we don't understand. Yet in real life it rewards well.

Most of us go through life spending on ourselves, saving for ourselves, and leaving all our money to our children to spend on themselves when we are gone. That's not a winning philosophy. The truth about wealth is "Whoever dies with the most toys loses."

Jesus often spoke in parables—puzzles that most people did not understand. He told a story about a man about to go on a journey who entrusted his investments to three money managers. To one he gave $5,000, to another $2,000, to a third $1,000—each according to his abilities. Then he went out of town. The first money manager went to work and doubled the $5,000 investment to $10,000. The second doubled the $2,000 investment to $4,000. When the investor returned he said to each money manager, "Good work! You did your job well. From now on be my partner!"

But the third money manager carefully buried his boss's working capital in the ground. The investor was furious with him and said, "That's a terrible way to live. It's criminal to live cautiously like that! If you knew I was after the best, why did you do less than the least?

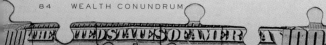

The least you could have done would have been to invest the sum with the bankers, where at least I would have gotten a little interest. Take the $1,000 and give it to the one who risked the most. And get rid of this 'play it safe' who won't go out on a limb. Throw him out into utter darkness."[22] Is this fair? Is God cruel? The third manager's motives may have been right in his own mind. He wanted to do what he thought his boss wanted. But he really didn't know his boss. That is how God sees our investment accounts. His goal is not for us to accumulate money but to accomplish His goals with it, just as the first two managers did. When we store up money in investment accounts instead of putting it to work, we are burying money in the ground.

THE MISINFORMED SERVANT
NEVER REALIZED THAT THE MONEY HIS BOSS
PLACED IN HIS HANDS TO MANAGE WASN'T
HIS HARVEST, BUT HIS SEED!

INVESTING IN PEOPLE

Jesus had a broader view of wealth than money accumulation. He was talking about investing everything you have to get the greatest return. That includes investing, but even more important, it means investing your life and whatever you have in people. That is commendable. That gives a reward that lasts.

I am in the investment business. I invest with the purpose of maximizing gains. I have an effective, well managed, profitable organization that produces profits that can be used in the most effective way possible.

> GIVING TO WORTHY CAUSES IS
> ANOTHER FORM OF COMPOUND INTEREST.
> I GET A HIGHER RATE OF RETURN WHEN I
> INVEST MY FUNDS IN PEOPLE AND
> IDEAS THAT PRODUCE A MULTIPLIER EFFECT
> THAN IF I KEPT THE MONEY FOR MYSELF
> AND GAVE IT AWAY LATER.

I give my money in the same way. My objective is to maximize the gain I can get by investing in society. What I give is multiplied in the outreach of the people who receive it, if I give wisely. Like a venture capital firm looking for places to give seed money with potentially big returns, I look for a potential multiplier effect in my giving.

I am an investor who combines business and ministry in order to maximize my returns. What I decided to do was a bit of both business and ministry. There is no dividing line between the secular and the

sacred. I am encouraged to allow God to lead and direct my business, entertainment, recreation, parenting, and church activities and integrate them together.

This is what I have attempted to accomplish in all my endeavors. Keeping God as the Boss of my life,

I attempt to do what He would want me to do in all my circumstances.

BUSINESS

An organization that provides a service with the objective of realizing a financial profit.

MINISTRY

An organization that provides a service without the objective of making a financial profit.

Permanent and Temporary Assets

You may remember that I said that the wealthy people I met in my estate planning service were some of the most unhappy people on earth. While I was helping them find out what they wanted in life and what they wanted to do with their money, I watched many family screaming matches. I saw fathers and sons battle it out, scrambling for wealth. I heard people shouting obscenities at one another. The more they hung onto their wealth, the more miserable they became.

I received a healthy perspective on how to look at money from Hank Bronson, a businessman and good friend. He sits with me on the board of trustees of the Haggai Institute, an organization that is one of the most effective organizations for evangelism and leadership training that I have found. Hank said that he keeps his financial statement up to date by listing his permanent assets separately from his temporary assets.

PERMANENT ASSETS

Money given away
(Value is added to the gifts for
time elapsed since giving)

TEMPORARY ASSETS

Stocks
Bonds
Real estate
Cash

Permanent assets include only what he has given away. When he computes the permanent value of the money he gives, he also uses a formula to incorporate a time value into that money. The funds he gave a long time ago are weighted with interest, and reflect a total present value.

Temporary assets include stocks and bonds, real estate, and the cash that he still controls.

Following in Hank's footsteps, I used his accounting method of giving and keeping until eventually my permanent net worth exceeded my temporary net worth.

I have also established a lifetime giving goal that intimidates and challenges me when I think about it. I posted it in a conspicuous place to remind me of its priority.

DR. JOHN EDMUND HAGGAI
HAS GIVEN ME A WALL PLAQUE THAT SAYS,
"ATTEMPT SOMETHING SO GREAT
FOR GOD IT'S DOOMED TO FAILURE
UNLESS GOD BE IN IT."

I always make a goal big enough to get excited about. Gifts to my foundation don't count. Gifts to my children don't count. Gifts left in my will don't count.

This is a lifetime goal. I want to die broke, keeping just enough seed money to be able to accomplish whatever God leads me to do.

If I give when I am alive, at least I know where it is going. Kenneth Keyes, a fundraiser who is the second largest realtor in the United States, said,

"Do your giving while you're living,
Then you're knowing where it's going."

How Much More Can I Find To Give Away?

A few years ago, my financial planning took on a new turn. I had spent the majority of my life reducing taxes and maximizing what I kept because I was a well qualified financial and estate planner. Over the years, my objective became very different, from how much I could keep for myself to how much I could give away.

By strategic planning, I learned how to give more to causes that were important to me. Not that paying income taxes is wrong, but when given the choice of who can make better use of the funds, I believe that organizations that I fund are more effective than organizations that the government funds, not to mention the issues of morality raised by certain government programs.

I applied all of the financial principles I knew to accomplish this. I would have strategy sessions with my lawyers and accountants to brainstorm ideas of how to maximize my giving every year. In fact, they found that it was fun and very creative to focus on new strategies different from all their other clients, who had the objective of accumulating more and more wealth.

Over the years, we have come up with several strategic giving methods to maximize what I donate to charitable causes. They include the following:

STRATEGIC GIVING METHODS

Professional services donated to charity

Liquidation of foundation assets immediately after death

Giving most of the principal while I'm alive

Brokerage margin account (borrowing funds to invest)

Giving beyond the tithe

Thinking like a steward because God owns it all

Professional services donated to charity. My foundation was set up in such a way that I could give away more of my income each year without having it subject to income tax. By volunteering my management services, I was able to direct income into the foundation that normally might have been taxable to me personally, and then distribute it without any income tax consequence. This is similar to the way an entertainer can perform at a benefit concert and not have any of the sales proceeds taxable to him.

Liquidation of foundation assets immediately after death. Many of the largest foundations (and universities,

for that matter) in this country were established by philanthropists whose primary objective was to spread the Christian Gospel, only to have funds after their death directed by board members to causes totally contrary to the founders' desires.

When I first set up a foundation, I wanted to be certain that my objectives would be accomplished in the event of my death, so I named a board of directors that represented most of the organizations where I was currently contributing. I had a liquidating arrangement in place that would terminate the foundation gradually and equally over a ten-year period following my death so that my objectives would still be in the minds of everyone on the board.

I was initially pleased about my willingness to cut the time of liquidation to ten years instead of allowing the board to hang on to the money until the purposes had become diluted from the things I wanted to accomplish. Eventually, however, I changed my mind to accelerate the entire foundation assets payout to within one year of my death. This insures that it will all go to causes that are currently effective.

Giving most of the principal while I'm alive. Shortly after that change, I decided that since it wasn't my money anyway, I needed to distribute the bulk of the foundation assets while I was alive, so I proceeded to give the vast majority of the principal away, keeping about 20 percent of the assets to invest and distribute to current needs. A few years ago, *Fortune* magazine carried a story about major philanthropists that compared the amount of money they had given away to what they kept. The lower the percentage of what they kept, the higher the magazine rated them as a giver.

Brokerage margin account (borrowing funds to invest). Another item I have used to maximize investment return on any investment funds remaining in the foundation was the use of a brokerage margin account. While many would think of this as risky, I have found that borrowing funds at low interest rates to invest using our trading systems has been quite profitable, even considering the bear market of 2000-2003.

There are times to be fully invested, and times to be in cash. When the time is right, borrowing to enhance returns is a wise idea. Although income tax had be paid on foundation profits attributed to borrowed money, I found it was worth it to earn more funds to give away.

Giving beyond the tithe. I always tithed, or gave the first 10 percent of my income to charity, but I see tithing in a new light now. Because everything belongs to God, I should consider how much I keep for myself as the issue, instead of how much I give. But more than just giving, tithing and giving beyond the tithe illustrates my relationship to the items that I possess.

Thinking like a steward because God owns it all. Now that I understood that God owns it all and I am just a steward, I felt more lighthearted and carefree, less possessive. And much more generous. It is a lot easier to give away someone else's money than my own!

JESUS WAS NOT POSSESSIVE ABOUT MONEY

We play a lot of games with MY and MINE. If I asked someone what they would do if they won a lottery worth millions of dollars, they would probably say they would give some of the proceeds to charity, but if they had to EARN the funds, they would likely not feel so inclined. How did Jesus show that He was not possessive about money?

Jesus made Judas the treasurer who kept the disciples' money bag. Judas was a thief! He stole from the bag whenever he needed anything.[23] Our Lord's ministry had such an abundance of funds that even with Judas as treasurer, who regularly stole from the account, there remained a sufficient financial surplus.

Jesus praised the woman who was so wasteful that she used up expensive perfume—worth a year's wages—on His feet.[24]

Jesus commended the widow who gave her last two pennies into the church treasury. He spoke well of her decision even though the temple priests were supposed to be caring for her, instead of vice versa.[25]

Many Bible references to money initially made no sense to me, like this one: "Give to everyone who asks of you. And from him who takes away your goods do not ask them back."[26] And this one: "If someone takes your coat, give him your shirt as well."[27] Tipping has become fun now that I realize that I am blessing someone. I used to dislike tipping, but now I am seeing it as another way to be generous in every area of my life.

I USED TO HAVE A PROBLEM FEELING "TAKEN ADVANTAGE OF" IN A FINANCIAL TRANSACTION UNTIL I REALIZED THAT IF I MADE A DECISION TO ALLOW THE OTHER PERSON TO TAKE ADVANTAGE OF ME, I COULD BLESS HIM IN A WAY THAT HE DIDN'T DESERVE.

No money is ever lost in a transaction, it just changes pockets. I need to remember this whenever I feel that someone has taken advantage of me. If I lived at the base of Niagara Falls and someone stole my cup of water, why should I be concerned? My focus should be having faith in the Source, not being distracted by the insignificant. I certainly did not want to do those things at first, but I had to relax and believe that Jesus might be right. He seemed to have a combination of penetrating criticism of wealth with a carefree, lighthearted attitude about possessions. How could I believe enough to act? How could I win the race against my greed?

22. Adapted from Matthew 25:14-29, *The Message*.

23. John 12:6.

24. Matthew 26:7-13; Mark 14:3-9; Luke 7:37-50; John 12:1-8.

25. Mark 12:42-44.

26. Luke 6:30-31 NKJV.

27. Luke 6:29 TLB.

Power is nothing without control.

EIGHT

RELAX AND WIN

DRIVING RACE CARS IS LIKE
THE CHRISTIAN LIFE.
IF YOU TRY TOO HARD YOU LOSE,
BUT IF YOU RELAX, YOU WIN.

Everyone gets a bit frightened for me when they hear about my passion for driving race cars. They ask, "How fast do you go?" Most of the time I don't know, because most race cars don't have speedometers, only tachometers. With racing it is not how fast you go that counts. It's how quickly you get around the track.

To some people, driving a race car doesn't seem like a Christian thing to do, and my dad still doesn't let me talk about it with him, but I want to dispel the notion that my spiritual life and my racing activities are not related. I have learned a lot about my relationship with God by driving race cars.

It's like the bumper sticker I saw that asked, "How would Jesus drive?" I believe He would drive very fast because He is in tune with God and understands the laws of physics. Jesus would be the best.

Several years ago, I decided I would buy a Twin Turbo Porsche. I had the money available, but since they were very rare at that time I had to shop around to find one to use for racing. After I made the decision, I decided to pray about it, thinking my request would just get rubber stamped for approval because I had the funds available. It didn't work out that way. Listening carefully to the Still Small Voice within, I was impressed that God said emphatically, NO!

When I asked Him why not, He said I wasn't good enough yet to use a car with that much power (over 400 hp). So I committed to learning to drive the car I had, an M5 BMW. I went to several driving schools, including Skip Barber and Bondurant, and worked hard on learning how to drive a medium-powered car. A year or two later, after I had forgotten all about my dream car, I was in a church worship service and out of nowhere I heard in my heart a message to go and get the Twin Turbo. Sometimes I think that God

laughs at all the religious stuff that people do. He just wants a relationship.

I try not to miss worship on Sunday mornings because it is the highlight of the week for me. This is when I can best hear directly from God, specifically to me, about the practical areas of my life.

The Porsche I really wanted was a 1997 Twin Turbo-S, the last of the air-cooled line of turbocharged Porsches that came with 424 horsepower right from the factory. It was a limited edition model that was available by special order. Reservations for these cars had to be placed within a 24-hour period with no advance notice given, and you had to put down a nonrefundable deposit of $20,000. I had missed the deadline, and found out that there would be only 180 of them made worldwide, and they were all sold.

Knowing how impossible it would be to find one, I asked a friend who referred me to a dealer in Florida who might know something about the car. I called about 6:30 P.M. and a sales rep picked up the phone. He laughed when I told him what I wanted.

He said that someone had canceled their order less than an hour before my call, and the sales team had just finished a meeting about it and they were all on the phones calling clients. He said that it would be sold within the hour. I told him it was mine and gave him my charge card number for a deposit. Hey, this is the way life is supposed to work!

God's timing, not my timing. No stress, no worry, no hurry, no guilt. Always being willing to let any deal

go without anxiety. Whether it is getting a new car, buying and selling real estate or hiring a new employee, I am learning to turn over all my decisions—both big and small—to God, and not to get obsessed with getting things I want immediately. I can wait for His timing, even though it is not an easy thing for me to do.

One thing I have learned. When someone tells me that I have to act quickly to buy something or it will be gone, I never buy on those terms. If God wants me to have it, it will be there after I have a chance to discuss it with Him. If I am all stressed out and in a hurry, I am probably not listening, but acting ahead of Him.

It turned out that this car was ideal for my introduction to racing with the Porsche Club of America, and I won several trophies in the Club Race series with it before converting it back to a street legal car, and purchasing an even faster (600 hp) race car.

Not In My Own Strength

Racing power

The key to driving fast is driving smoothly. If I attempt to drive the car in my own strength, I will be too slow. What do I mean by the phrase "in my own strength"? I have to remember that this car weighs 3,000 pounds.

Laws of physics determine how fast it can get around the track. God created these rules and they are not negotiable. My problem is trying too hard to take the car around the track. When my hand muscles ache, or I tense up and stomp my foot down to the floor, I know I am pushing too hard with my own strength. I end up not driving as fast as when I relax. I need to listen to the car.

YOU CAN GO AROUND A CORNER
JUST SO FAST WITHOUT LEAVING THE ROAD
SURFACE. ONE MILE-AN-HOUR FASTER
AND YOU WILL RUN TWO WHEELS
OFF THE PAVEMENT AND INTO THE DIRT.
MAYBE ALL FOUR WHEELS.

Feel the car. Let the engine do the work. Relax. Don't grab the wheel so hard. Be smooth. Make small adjustments. Listen to what the car is saying to you. Listen to the tires. Look where you want to go.

Then I go faster.

This is easy to talk about, but hard to do. Driving a race car well requires more skill, knowledge, and practice than any other sport I have ever attempted, and it is less forgiving when I don't listen.

SURFING POWER

Racing cars and surfing—especially at my hotel in Costa Rica—are my two favorite activities, and they are very much alike. In surfing, the power is in the wave. I initiate the paddle to catch the wave, and make small adjustments of balance along the ride to stay in the right place on the wave so that I don't get into trouble. If I tense up and try too hard, I lose my

connection with the wave and my balance is affected, with potentially unpleasant results.

SPIRITUAL POWER

The same principles apply to my spiritual life. I listen. I hear what God says. I agree and confess my shortcomings. I follow His rules. I relax and let Him change me. I set the direction and He provides the power.

The key to an abundant Christian life is letting God change me from the inside out. The apostle Paul says in his letter to the Romans to "present your bodies a living sacrifice."[28] I offer myself to Him just the way I am. He begins doing the work to change me. I agree to His rules, and He changes me into someone I like better.

Ron Blue said it this way: "God merely wants you to take the first step, then the second step, then the third step, so that when you stand before Him, you will finally understand that whatever has been accomplished has been accomplished by Him."

Giving things up once you have them may be even harder to do than buying them. One Sunday morning recently during a fund raising campaign for our new church building, I felt God asking me to give not just money, but also a sacrifice. As I searched my list of prize possessions, my Twin Turbo S Porsche sifted up to the top. I felt that He was asking me to give it back, so I sold it and donated the funds. I need to think of all my possessions in the "on loan" category.

The love of money and the love of possessions are spiritual forces that become energized as I turn my affections on them. If I think of money as something belonging to God that He has given to me to manage, it retains its proper perspective in my life. It's His money, with my name on the account. I'm His steward, managing His resources.

I believe that I'm God's steward, and most of the time I try to act like His steward, but I still have struggles with this arrangement. In the next chapter, I'll share some of the struggles I have had.

28. Romans 12:1 NKJV.

NINE

STEWARDSHIP STRUGGLES

EVEN WHEN YOU WANT TO GIVE,
YOUR OWN UNANSWERED QUESTIONS
CAN DIVERT YOU UNLESS YOU HAVE FAITH.

I once was in charge of a Bible study where I was trying to explain to a small group of friends the meaning of stewardship. As an experiment, I gave each of the attendees a $100 bill with an assignment for the following week. I told them, "This money does not belong to you. It does not belong to me. This is God's money. You have one week to look at your situation and put it to use someplace where you think God would be pleased.

"You will try to have God's eyes this week. I want you to do something with this money that He leads you to do. Next week you will be accountable to report back what you did with it."

Well, the next week not everyone came back, but it certainly had an impact on those who did. By faith, I am hoping that they got some return on it, and now view their money from a fresh perspective.

IF IT ALL BELONGS TO GOD . . .

Stewardship, as you recall, means that all of what I "own" belongs to God, and I am just His steward. I guess we all wrestle with that. Over the years I have tried to understand the implications of that relationship and find answers to my stewardship questions. Sometimes I come up with answers that are illogical to me, but maybe that is the basis for faith. Eventually I have to stop looking for answers, even in the Bible, and simply act on my beliefs, uncomfortable or not. I have to step out in faith.

I have an employee who runs my business for me. She has authority to write checks and spend company funds for things that benefit the company. She is my steward, and acts in a manner where she represents me and my objectives in the operation of my business. How would I feel if she decided to cut

herself a big check and take a family vacation in Hawaii with corporate funds?

STEWARDS MAINTAIN A VERY
POWERFUL POSITION: THEY MAINTAIN
ACCESS TO EVERYTHING,
WHILE ACTUALLY OWNING NOTHING.

If I ask the same question of my own financial stewardship under God I get a better perspective.

"O.K., God, what should I do in this situation? Spend, invest, or give it away?"

My mentor, Evangelist Tommy Tyson, at one time considered joining a commune where everyone owned their property in common. God prompted him to take his wallet out of his pocket and count the money inside, asking him where he got the funds. Acknowledging that it was a gift from Him, he felt God say to him, "If you will accept everything as a gift from Me, and you are willing to use it as I guide you, then I don't mind if you carry it in your own pocket."

This concept has been helpful to me regarding the material things that I own. For example, if I had a rental car that was stolen, I probably wouldn't get very upset, just report it to the authorities and get another

one. But if "MY" car was stolen . . . ? If only I could have this mindset for all my possessions.

QUESTIONS I HAVE ASKED MYSELF

Should I tithe only my taxable income? Should I tithe the net or the gross? What about the appreciation of my IRA or unrealized real estate gains?

Should I give away more than a tithe?

How do I give 50 percent by the end of each year (the IRS 50 percent contribution rule)?

Should I continue to compound the wealth and increase my retirement plan, or give more away?

What is the purpose of my retirement plan if I don't plan on retiring?

If I can't take it with me, can I send it on ahead for eternal rewards?

Does money left to charity at my death count toward eternal rewards?

As a steward of what God has entrusted to me, should I leave money to my children?

Why did Jesus let Judas keep the treasury funds, knowing that he could steal whenever he pleased?

SHOULD I GIVE TO ANYONE WHO REQUESTS
    MONEY?

HOW DO I OVERCOME MY CHRONIC STICKY
    FINGERS SYNDROME?

HOW DO I DEFEAT THE HOARDING TACTICS OF
    "DELAY, DIVERSION, AND DISCORD"?

Should I tithe only my taxable income? Should I tithe the net or the gross? What about the appreciation of my IRA or unrealized real estate gains? How about tax free municipal bond income? What about growth of my IRA retirement account? What about the increase in value in my home? Most taxes are levied when an asset is sold and the gain is realized. But what about a realized gain in my retirement plan? What about tithing an inheritance? You can see where this kind of legalism can lead. The Bible says to tithe on the *"firstfruits of all your increase."* [29] That is an agricultural term that seems to indicate that the growth of my assets should be included in my income, and it should be tithed.

The Bible says, "The purpose of tithing is to teach you always to put God first in your lives." [30] Tithing affects everything else in your life. Jesus said if you are not faithful with money, then God will not bless you with spiritual blessings. [31] That indicates that your giving and your spiritual life are very much connected.

The Bible has some extreme language for people who do not tithe:

> *"And now you're under a curse—the whole lot of you—because you're robbing me. Bring your full tithe to the Temple treasury so there will be ample provisions in my Temple. Test me in this and see if I don't open up heaven itself to you and pour out blessings beyond your wildest dreams."* [32]

Tithing is one of God's tests to see clearly if we put Him first. It sets in motion a law of reciprocity that brings prosperity. It is a basic fundamental law with spiritual consequences. Tithing from the firstfruits of your increase requires an element of faith, since it wouldn't require any faith if you paid tithes only if you had some funds left over after spending the rest.

I heard a story from a minister who asked his associate pastor why he was not tithing. His response was interesting, but flawed. He said that when he took the position as associate pastor he gave up a job that paid three times as much. According to his theology, he was already giving 200 percent, even though he was not giving anything. We need to be faithful in what we *have* been given, not with what we *could* have been given.

Most people say they would give if they won the lottery. That is putting things backward. Does the farmer say, "When someone fills up my barn, then I will plant the seed"? No, he plants the small amount of seed that he has, and then reaps a crop from it. Then he plants more and reaps more. It is an exponential formula that works for giving just as compound interest works for investments.

GIVING STARTS AN
EXPONENTIAL CYCLE OF BLESSING.

Should I give away more than a tithe? I found out over the years that the more I gave, the more I made. When I began giving more than ten percent, the blessings really began to roll.

As I mentioned earlier, you can think of giving in terms of seed. How much seed should you plant? Well, how much fruit do you want to reap? Put God to the test with tithing. Ask others who have done it. Gradually increase each year from 10 percent, to 20 percent, to 30 percent, and watch what happens. One man increased his tithe by one percent each year, and each year his disposable income went up.

It doesn't matter how much or how little you have, tithing will prosper everyone at every socio-economic level, even those who think they have nothing. Yes, that means everyone, without exception.

Consider this challenge from Bob Shank: "Speculation—if the tithe is God's by mandate, there is a case to be made that the only funds deposited in your name in heaven are those discretionary gifts that go beyond the first-fruits of the tithe!" I haven't heard this from the pulpit either. But it is something to think about.

How do I give 50 percent by the end of each year? As a financial planner, if I had a retirement plan where I could deposit up to 50 percent of my income and deduct it on my income tax, wouldn't I be foolish not to? I might cash in other investments or assets that I could live on while I was funding the plan.

If I am a steward of assets that all belong to God, then I need to take advantage of the full tax deduction allowable for charitable contributions. This deduction is currently limited to 50 percent of my adjusted gross income. Once the tax year goes by, if I have not taken advantage of the 50 percent limit, I can never use it again in the future. Ever since I figured that out, I have attempted to give away at least 50 percent of my adjusted gross income each year, even if inconvenient. Use it or lose it. Some years I had to take out a loan to fund gifts due to a cash flow problem, but I didn't want to miss that opportunity. For the year 2005, there was a one-time exception to this rule. Tax legislation passed to encourage Hurricane Katrina relief efforts increased the gift limit to 100 percent of adjusted gross income for that year for gifts to any charitable organization.

Should I continue to compound the wealth and increase in my retirement plan, or give more away? As a result of one of the biggest bull markets of the century, my retirement assets have grown tax-free over the past two decades to one hundred times what I originally invested, even though I stopped making contributions long ago. I have much more than I need for my retirement income.

For many years, I was able to annually draw from this retirement account an amount to give away without income tax penalty, subject to annuity rules issued by the IRS, even though I was not yet 59 and a half years old. (At age 59 and a half the rules currently allow unlimited retirement plan withdrawals without penalty.)

Why shouldn't I pull it all out and give it away? Well, I still hate to pay taxes, and if I pulled it out of my IRA, I would only be able to deduct 50 percent, due to the income tax law limitation mentioned above. I would have to pay tax on the other half even if I gave it all away. On the other hand, if you are not giving at the 50 percent level, you could pay out from your IRA up to 50 percent of your adjusted gross income and still deduct it.

As a result of the current tax laws, I have unfortunately created an artificial mind barrier to cashing out more of the retirement funds because of my excuse that I would have to pay taxes on what I gave. This is an unfortunate rule in current tax law that may someday be changed by legislation, but I am still struggling with it. There are many needy people who could use this money, but I have regrettably decided that they are not important enough for me to pay taxes on these funds to get them distributed to the people.

Meanwhile, I am waiting until I can donate the retirement funds without having to pay a tax penalty.

However, I know that if one of my children needed expensive surgery, you better believe I would cash out some funds. I wouldn't care if I had to pay the tax if they needed the money. So there seems to be a lack of integrity here in my thinking. I have rationalized that since most of my retirement funds are able to go to charity tax-free at my death, then that solves the issue. It remained a cause of unrest that I continued to debate while compound interest grew my retirement funds into a big pile of cash. My dilemma was finally resolved by taking advantage of the tax legislation passed to encourage Hurricane Katrina Relief efforts in 2005 when I was able to transfer most of my retirement account to charitable organizations without any federal income tax consequences.

I CERTAINLY CANNOT ADVISE ANYONE ON HOW MUCH IS ENOUGH TO SET ASIDE FOR RETIREMENT, BUT THERE CERTAINLY IS A BALANCING ISSUE BETWEEN THE NEED TO TAKE CARE OF OUR FAMILIES IN THE FUTURE AND THE NEED TO GIVE TO WORTHY CAUSES NOW.

What is the purpose of my retirement plan if I don't plan to retire? If God promises to provide for my future, why am I hoarding money for retirement? It seems to go back to my estate planning philosophy. Save it for later. Don't pay taxes. Amass wealth. My estate plan designates that any remaining retirement funds will go to charity by beneficiary designation when I die.

No income or estate taxes are currently payable if I do it that way. That sounds like my temporal value system motivating me.

If I can't take it with me, can I send it on ahead for eternal rewards? I never heard about the concept of rewards after death until later in my life, but Jesus referred to it many times. He said that those who give up things for Him "will receive now in return, a hundred times over, houses, brothers, sisters, mothers, children, and property—with persecutions. And in the world to come they will have eternal life." [33]

"This is once again the Great Reversal: Many who are first will end up last, and the last first." [34]

This would seem to be a permanent retirement plan as opposed to a temporary one, with a promise of hundredfold returns. So why don't I take the money out of my retirement account, pay the tax, and give away the remainder so that God can reward me, now and in the life to come? Is paying taxes really that bad? Isn't it possibly just another way to give to the poor?

Does money left to charity at my death count toward eternal rewards? I heard an encouraging yet controversial message by Bruce Wilkinson, author of the bestseller *The Prayer of Jabez.* He seems to have great insight and integrity in his spiritual and business life, but he said something that initially I could not accept. He said that money that is left to charity when you die may not qualify for an eternal reward, but be lost.

I have thought a lot about that since I heard it. My analytical mind has been stirring up this concept, and it seems to me that charity would get more if I left my money at death since there would be no taxes to reduce what was given. My expended life would be the trigger that would set in motion the funding, but my estate would be the giver. "I" would not be giving it. Good point, although not conclusive, causing me to continue to struggle with this concept without answers.

And then there is also the issue of leaving things at my death with instructions that may never be carried out. There could be lawyers, lawsuits, probate, contestability issues, and organizations that are no longer effective. Those are reasons enough to give while I'm alive, not to mention that I can enjoy seeing the gifts actually doing something. I can see lives

changed, the hungry being fed, children getting the medical attention they need, and scholarships being given to train the next generation of believers.

A dollar invested now may be worth hundreds later. If you give money to train one person who will train a hundred others, the increase is much greater than giving much later when you die. Think how many kernels of corn you could have if you planted today and continued to plant the harvest each year. If one kernel reproduces only 100 more each year, in ten years the final crop will be one hundred quintillion kernels, or 1 with 20 zeros.

As a steward of what God has entrusted to me, should I leave money to my children? Coming from an estate planning background, I had learned all the tools of wealth transfer, and I learned how to eliminate virtually all estate taxes through trusts and generation-skipping techniques. Very few clients I worked for had the objective of giving to anyone other than their children or grandchildren, so my stewardship concept was beginning to cause me to rethink these same issues. I asked myself this question: "Does my bank trust officer, who is a 'steward' of my estate, leave my estate assets to HIS children when he dies?" No!

There are two main issues at stake here. One is the assumed obligation that my children should be entitled to my remaining assets when I die. The other is whether or not it will be good for them if they do inherit it. Maybe I love them enough to *not* leave them wealth. Gandhi preached about a list of seven social sins, one of which was "Wealth Without Work," and another, "Worship Without Sacrifice."

Reviewing the stewardship principles, I asked myself questions like these:

"Do my children have the same value system as I do?"

"Would they use the money in a way that God would approve?"

I remember the first time I sat down with my five children, the average age being in the late teens. I wanted to introduce them to the concept of getting involved in seeking out areas of need in the community and to get them thinking about philanthropic endeavors. I was shocked to find out that they didn't even know what a charitable organization was, and, like most teenagers, they really had little interest in finding out more.

Teaching children about wealth and financial responsibility are an important part of parenting. Age, maturity, and sensitivity in handling funds are an important consideration in determining their level of involvement. A large sum of money left in the hands

of a young person might be the worst thing a parent could do for them, especially when they are becoming career minded and seeking to become educated. It can divert them from their "call" in life and deprive them of the lessons they need to learn firsthand, walking by faith, and allowing God to provide for them.

Watching children make mistakes may be one of the most difficult things that a parent has to do, but ultimately it should speed up their learning curve.

I will always save the note my daughter sent to me when she first got married to thank me for teaching her the simple financial principle of paying cash for items and avoiding credit card debt, while she watched her friends financially crash and burn.

Why did Jesus let Judas keep the treasury funds, knowing that he could steal whenever he pleased? How would you feel if your pastor did the same? Jesus showed that He was not possessive about money when He made Judas the treasurer who kept the disciples' money bag.[35] Jesus was always telling people to give their money to the poor, even though they might misuse it. He rebuked the man who asked him to settle a financial dispute with his brother, saying he needed to check out his heart motives (greed).[36] Was that a fair comment? I am still working on this one, since it does not seem fair, but Jesus went straight to the heart of important issues.

Should I give to anyone who requests money? Although Jesus said in the Sermon on the Mount to give to anyone who asks of you,[37] I need to check with Him prayerfully before anyone gets anything. I am aware that everyone is barraged by requests for money. I have determined that what works best for me is to give to only a few effective ministries, rather than scattering my money in shotgun giving. As I said earlier, I approach giving like a venture capitalist, finding the most effective ministries by due diligence and giving only a few of them a substantial amount of money, instead of giving small amounts to many organizations that I have not evaluated. Normally I have a leading to give to a cause before I am even approached, although I still need to be sensitive to the needs of others who approach me.

I want to feel as if my contribution is making a difference. I give to causes that Jesus would approve of, like evangelization of the Gospel (which creates a dependence on God and a relationship with God in determining life's decisions), taking care of the needy, and helping people to become financially independent.

After reading the book *Rambam's Ladder* by Julie Salamon, which discusses eight levels of philanthropy, I have attempted to give at the top level, which is giving to help people become independent. I look for a multiplication factor, also, where each dollar makes a

major difference and yields a return, just like a financial investment. Giving as God prompts me also relieves any guilt in not giving to all causes. I need to remember these funds are His funds, and I am just directing them as He leads me.

How do I overcome my chronic sticky fingers syndrome? I still have difficulty parting with money. My nature encourages me to pile it up and compound it into a nice big cash endowment.

I sit on the board of directors of several organizations. One of my contributions is to encourage ministries to use their benevolence funds now and not accumulate large endowments. In general, I prefer not to contribute to an organization's endowment fund, but to give to a specific operational need, since excess funds in the treasury of a worthy organization won't do any more good than excess funds in my own foundation.

In fact, in order to counteract the hoarding problem that is quite widespread in the Christian community, I encourage everyone to be accountable to a board of directors with their personal finances. There is nothing wrong with an operating cash reserve, or setting up a fund to accumulate for a known need, but there is nothing enviable about the spiritual staleness of a large church with such a big endowment that there is no incentive for the people to give.

People need to give for their own spiritual health. Endowments create complacency and deny the opportunity to see God prove that He can meet the needs of His people. People need to give to be blessed.

How do I defeat the hoarding tactics of "Delay, Diversion, and Discord"? On the telephone in my office is a sticker that reads "Delay, Diversion, Discord." These are the things that block my giving and cause me to keep funds in my own pocket. Be on the lookout for these tactics of the enemy in your own life that keep you from giving.

GIVING DEFEATS DEPRESSION

Over the past few years, when I have been short of cash, or discouraged, or events have gone wrong, or spiritual attacks have come against me, the first thing I have done is go to my temporary investment account and send out checks to charitable organizations that Jesus would support. My first response after the terrorist attack on the World Trade Center was to immediately send a check to a cause that I felt could best solve the problem. It is my way of going on the offensive and putting into action the law of reciprocity.

I once had my briefcase stolen while traveling outside the country. Inside were many valuable items, including my passport. At first I felt anger, but then I

realized that because of the stewardship principle it wasn't really my briefcase. I was able to relax and laugh a bit, especially because there was a book inside entitled *Money, Possessions and Eternity* by Randy Alcorn. I hoped the thief would read it and realize his shortsightedness! As a result of this loss, I bought a new briefcase, better than the old one, and purchased other new items to put inside. Then I also was able to take a few extra days of vacation as I waited for a new passport, making lemonade from the sour lemons I had been given.

Life is not all about money. It's about what you do with what God has given you. That is one of the lessons I have been learning in the search for financial freedom. While true financial freedom is found only in total dependence on God, living in a fallen world gives us the need to use money.

I still have a lot of questions about the practical issues of dealing with money, and I certainly don't have all the answers. It seems that money is a necessity in our current economic environment. Money itself is not good or bad. The way it is used determines that.

Every piece of currency includes the words "Federal Reserve Note." The piece of paper that we call money is nothing more than a debt instrument issued by the U. S. government. If I burn a five dollar

bill, it is not an act of treason, but an act of forgiveness by me toward all the other U.S. citizens who owe me the five bucks.

One day I went to the bank, got $10,000 worth of cash in hundred dollar bills, and did the thing that everyone has always wanted to do but never did. I threw the wad of bills up in the air into my bedroom ceiling fan and watched them float around the room. Unfortunately, the gas fireplace was lit and one of the bills landed right on a burning log.

Let's just call it forgiveness of debt, not foolishness.

SOME OF MY WEALTH CAN BE SPENT

Some people might call foolishness my occasional lavish spending on things like expensive cars and a nice home. After all, Mother Teresa certainly had no use for a race car. But the God I serve is a big God Who loves me, and wants me to prosper and have an abundant life in every way, including the things I love to do most.

"Delight yourself also in the Lord, and He shall give you the desires of your heart."[38]

"You shall not muzzle an ox while it treads out the grain."[39]

If I had a partner who worked with me and helped produce profits, why would I condemn him for using some of the profits for himself? He could have

been out playing golf or watching TV, but instead he is making profits for me.

If I knew how much pleasure a new purchase would bring him, I would be glad for him to use some of the profits he generated.

That's how God views our partnership. The Bible does not teach that we should all have the same amount of wealth, as some well meaning "justice socialists" would have you believe, but it teaches that God will supply our needs and prosper us.

People who take a vow of poverty may have overlooked the obvious: eliminating the opportunity to access money does not cure the underlying spirit of greed, it just gives people a new set of problems. Jesus didn't tell everyone to renounce all they possess, only those whose possessions kept them from God. We all have to obey the first commandment—No other gods before Him!

Faithful stewardship dictates that all ownership of material goods is surrendered, and that everything we control is the property of God. Faithful stewardship trumps a vow of poverty.

WEALTH-BUILDING PRINCIPLES

The principles of building wealth that you will find in the next chapter have worked well for me. Anyone

who applies them will move quickly toward wealth and financial independence. Once a person comes to the place where his passive investment income is equal to his expenses, he has more freedom to give to support others who need help. There is one caveat: we need to stay open at all times to giving back all of our financial independence to God if He asks for it.

29. Proverbs 3:9 NKJV.

30. Deuteronomy 14:23 TLB.

31. Luke 16:11.

32. Malachi 3:9-10 *The Message.*

33. Mark 10:29-30 NLT.

34. Mark 10:31 *The Message.*

35. John 12:6. See also Chapter 7 of *Wealth Conundrum.*

36. Luke 12:13-15.

37. Matthew 5:42.

38. Psalm 37:4 NKJV.

39. Deuteronomy 25:4 NKJV.

TEN

A LIFE OF FINANCIAL FREEDOM

ANYONE CAN ACHIEVE A LIFE OF
FINANCIAL FREEDOM IF THEY
UNDERSTAND HOW TO PLAY THE GAME.

Over the years I have learned not to make it my sole object in life to accumulate great wealth. However, I have achieved some success in discovering wealth-building rules that work even for those not yet ready to begin a lifestyle of giving. I wish someone had told me about them when I started out.

Financial freedom is a common desire of everyone, but like everything else there is a right way and a wrong way to go about it. How you take

133

the journey determines the quality of life you experience once you get there. The Bible speaks of generational blessings resulting from making right choices, and curses resulting from making wrong choices. Each generation learns from parents and grandparents both good and bad habits. Patterns of generosity and blessing can be passed down, and also patterns of poverty and joblessness. You will reap what you sow. If you are a generous person, it will come back to you. If you are self-serving and stingy, that has consequences, too.

> One man gives freely, yet gains even more;
> another withholds unduly, but comes
> to poverty.[40]

This last verse says generous giving contributes to abundance while withholding leads to scarcity.

Looking For Ways To Be Generous

Many people are not convinced that giving should be a way of life. I was once in that camp in a major way. I couldn't have been much more tightfisted. However, after studying the teaching of Jesus and working alongside Mother Teresa, I began my Seven-Year Turn to the giving lifestyle. Now I attempt to look for ways to be generous. Faith for giving develops slowly but surely. Once financial independence is achieved, giving becomes easier for many to implement.

STEPS TO A LIFE
OF FINANCIAL FREEDOM

Dedicate your possessions to God.

Start early.

Set personal financial goals.

Give the first ten percent.

Pay yourself before spending.

Get rich slowly.

Be patient.

Lotteries are for losers.

Spend less than you earn.

Establish a budget.

Compound your interest.

Use IRA and other tax-deferred investments.

Never borrow to buy a depreciating asset.

Don't buy a car until you first save the money.

Borrow money only for investments or home mortgages.

Stay out of debt.

Minimize risk by diversification.

Minimize losses, maximize gains.

PROTECT YOUR WEALTH WITH INSURANCE.

CONSIDER CHARITABLE TRUSTS.

Dedicate your possessions to God. Dr E. Stanley Jones used to say, "A road that perhaps more than any other leads to self-atrophy is undedicated money."

Start early. It cannot be emphasized enough the impact that time has on compound interest. Get started early. Don't wait. If you're going to need lumber when you are 65, you don't want to plant the acorns when you are 50.

Set personal financial goals. Each person needs to set personal financial goals, and then establish a plan to achieve them. Determine what you want to do with your wealth, how much you will need, and when you will need it. Then begin planning carefully what income streams you will use to produce that wealth.

THE ONLY ANTIDOTE TO MATERIALISM

IS GIVING, BECAUSE IT IS

EXACTLY THE OPPOSITE OF GREED.

Give the first ten percent. When you receive income, the first thing I would recommend that you do is to start tithing. Give the first 10 percent back to God.

Since the Bible teaches that the tithe belongs to God, you need to give it where He directs you to give—to your local church where you are spiritually fed, or to the poor or less fortunate if you do not belong to one. This simple principle puts God first and squashes the spirit of greed and materialism, a foe that does not lie down and die easily. Giving disarms the controlling spirit of Mammon.

In his book *The God Account,* Robert M. Benedict gives a practical way of handling tithes and offerings. After "falling on his face financially," he read in Malachi where God challenges us to put Him to the test by giving Him the full tithe.

> *"Bring all the tithes into the storehouse,*
> *That there may be food in My house,*
> *And try Me now in this,"*
> *Says the LORD of hosts,*
> *"If I will not open for you the windows*
> *of heaven*
> *And pour out for you such blessing*
> *That there will not be room enough to*
> *receive it."* [41]

Benedict accepted God's challenge and established a separate "God Account" checking account, each

month depositing the 10 percent tithe (and offerings above that) BEFORE depositing the remainder of the income in his own checkbook. Then he and his wife pray, "God, where do You want Your money to go?" Over the last 22 years, they have had some of the most meaningful spiritual adventures of their lives—and God has bountifully blessed their financial situation. The dedicated "God Account" has provided practical help to many people.

Pay yourself before spending. The next principle is to "pay yourself" by setting aside some of your income in a separate account before that money becomes accessible for expenses. This could be a retirement or investment account that is not easily accessible so it does not turn into a "deferred spending" account. After the tithe, I recommend setting aside a minimum of 10 to 20 percent of income for personal investment. Then go ahead and enjoy spending and giving away the rest! This percentage will vary depending on age and family situation, but 10 to 20 percent of income should be a benchmark.

Get rich slowly. The basic concept of wealth building is to build it slowly. Avoid get-rich-quick schemes. The faster you try to get rich, the quicker you lose money on risky ventures. Each of my newsletters includes a Proverb by one of the wealthiest men who ever lived, Solomon:

Steady plodding brings prosperity;
hasty speculation brings poverty. [42]

Be patient. Time is a necessary ingredient for investments to work in your favor. Your investment may start out as small as an acorn, but it increases by a certain percentage each year, and eventually through exponential growth it's a mighty oak tree. If you stand watching a teakettle, it takes forever to boil, but if you walk away and do something else, before you know it, it whistles!

EVERY PERSON ALIVE CAN BE FINANCIALLY INDEPENDENT IF THEY TAKE THE RIGHT ACTIONS, AND TAKE RESPONSIBILITY FOR THEIR OWN DESTINY.

Investments work the same way. When your money is invested, stop watching it and enjoy life instead of worrying about it every day. Before you know it, the funds will double, and then double again.

Lotteries are for losers. Lotteries are one of the largest revenue generators for state governments, and participants, in their ignorance, don't seem to mind contributing. The lottery contributes to the inherited curse of entitlement programs. It plays on the mindset of getting something for nothing. Whenever I see someone buying a lottery ticket, I feel badly for them and wish I could help them understand this principle: Regular saving will make everyone wealthy, given enough time, but lotteries are for losers.

Spend less than you earn. This stewardship concept seems simple in theory, but plays havoc with our lives when we have a "natural" mindset. Normally, if we have the money and want something, we buy it. We have to help ourselves save by putting some money out of reach.

NO MILLIONAIRE ON THIS PLANET GOT THAT WAY BY SPENDING 100 PERCENT OF THE MONEY HE OR SHE MADE.

Record your expenses. A key to accountability is keeping track of where you spend your money. When I got my first job, my wife and I kept a logbook where we kept track of every dollar that we spent. I mean literally every dollar. If you don't know where your money is going, you can't figure out how to spend less, how to budget, and how to save.

Establish a budget. A budget will keep your funds going where you want them to go. Software accounting programs like Quicken and others can help you organize your money.

Compound your interest. The two words COMPOUND INTEREST should be capitalized whenever used together. Compound interest is a secret of wealth that very few people understand. Principal (money), time, and rate of growth come together in such a dynamic force that if one could live long enough, and maintain a steady growth rate, he would end up with all the money in the world. Did you ever wonder why all the rich people are old? It's compound interest!

Albert Einstein said compound interest is the greatest mathematical discovery of all time, not $E=mc^2$.

Use IRA and other tax-deferred investments. A tax deferred investment account is a powerful concept over time. An IRA or company retirement plan is a good idea because earnings on the investment are not subject to taxes as the money grows. (The contributions may also be deductible against current income.) For example, $10,000 placed into an IRA earning 10 percent interest will be worth $174,000 in 30 years if the earnings are not subject to annual income taxes, but worth only $76,000 if in a taxable account subject to taxation in a 30 percent tax bracket.

IF A COLLEGE GRADUATE INVESTED IN AN IRA ALL THE MONEY HE WOULD OTHERWISE HAVE SPENT ON HIS FIRST NEW CAR, WHEN HE TURNED AGE 65 HE WOULD BE A MILLIONAIRE, EVEN AFTER ADJUSTING FOR INFLATION.

Maximize your contribution to any qualified retirement program such as a 401k, particularly if there is an employer matching contribution. Annuities (both fixed and variable) are a good tax-deferred investment idea. Unlike a qualified retirement IRA, which has contribution limits, there are no limits on how much can be invested in an investment annuity. A Roth IRA also fits in this tax-free category, where funds are not deductible when invested, but grow tax-free, and are also tax-free when paid out. This should be one of the first investments most young people should consider.

Never borrow to buy a depreciating asset. People who use charge cards to purchase things and pay 12 to 20 percent interest rates will forever live in poverty. My longstanding rule of financial prosperity has always been "never borrow money to purchase anything that does not increase in value." If you don't have the money, don't buy it. Pray for it, save for it, and wait until God brings it into your life. Waiting builds your faith and your relationship with God as He proves Himself as a Provider. Use credit cards only for convenience and *pay them off in full each month.*

Don't buy a car until you first save the money. One time I was searching the classifieds for a used car and saw an ad looking for someone to take over car payments. When I called and asked how much cash he wanted for the car, he said he didn't know. He only knew what the payments were, and he probably owed more than the value of the car. Don't buy a car until you have saved enough to pay for it. An exception for this may be if the car is used for business to generate income or if needed to get to work, but newer used cars can be cost-effective.

Borrow money only for investments or home mortgages. Borrowing funds to purchase higher yielding assets may make sense if you are able to evaluate the risks involved. One example would be purchasing a piece of income-producing property where the income exceeds the debt service. This concept can create wealth if the property appreciates over time. However, if your tenant moves out, you must assume the risk of making the payments on the loan, as well as potentially watching the property drop in value.

Home mortgage debt may be the one exception that I would suggest to people who are disciplined and able to invest wisely. By taking out a long-term, low-interest, tax-deductible mortgage and by creating a separate side investment fund instead of paying off the mortgage early, you can eventually be in a position to pay off the debt if you choose. Meanwhile, you will be earning income by investing separately with your other funds. Of course, this will only work if you don't spend the funds and if you earn a higher return on your investment than the interest you are paying for your mortgage.

I recognize that many people may be more comfortable having no debt, as it certainly does give a more secure feeling to have no mortgage payments. But if you have the option of paying off the mortgage at any time, you are not putting yourself into a position of having to make payments from wages. Each person's financial freedom number is reached when passive income is equal to expenses.

Stay out of debt. Other than exceptions like the investment use of debt noted above, stay out of debt. If you stay out of debt, you will never become enslaved to lenders. As the Bible says in Proverbs, "The borrower is servant to the lender."[43] If you are already in debt, you need to work out a plan to get out as soon as possible. Howard Dayton's book *Your Money Counts* gives practical methods to do just that. It is a classic biblical guide to earning, spending, saving, budgeting, investing, and giving. I highly recommend it. It also covers important issues such as training your children in these four areas: routine responsibilities, exposure to work, earning extra money at home, and working for others. A small group study is also available with this book in most metropolitan areas in the U.S. through Crown Ministries.

Minimize risk by diversification. By diversification— using several different investment strategies simultaneously—risk can be significantly reduced. Don't put all of your investment eggs in one basket. Build a portfolio of diverse investments like stocks, bonds, real estate and possibly other investment vehicles. If you ran a business and made only one product, you would be very vulnerable to market swings. Everything would have to go perfectly. It never does. If you have real estate, diversify geographically. If you live in a town with one factory or the community is heavily dependent on one industry or government influence, there may be more risk involved than meets the eye.

Diversify stocks and bonds by various trading strategies. Personally, I have found that "buy and hold" investing subjects me to more risk than I am willing to take, so I have implemented various trading strategies that reduce risk. By doing this I have personally escaped the Bear markets of 1987, 1990, and 2002 with minimal losses, keeping most of the gains of the prior Bull markets. If you want to send supplies down a fast running river, you can put it all on one big raft, or send it down on five smaller ones. If you lose one, you have four left.

Minimize losses, maximize gains. Don't be afraid to take small losses. In fact, in my investment business I take many more losses than gains because I keep them small and let the profits run. If you sell your winners too quickly and your losers too slowly, you will eventually end up holding all losers. Remember, if you lose 50 percent of your money in a bad investment, you need to get a 100 percent return just to get back to even, so minimizing losses is one of the first principles of wealth building. A 75 percent loss requires a 300 percent gain to return to the original investment.

A drawdown is an investment term for temporarily losing money. Everyone has drawdowns, whether they are aware of them or not. Some people think that if they buy a stock that goes down in price that they do not have a loss until they sell it. They are wrong. Markets adjust constantly, and losses are one of the guaranteed aspects of investing.

The key to success is to minimize losses and maximize gains. You will take losses, but keeping losses small and gains large is the key to success. Sometimes it is a challenge to find an advisor who can do that for you. Everyone talks about the stock they bought at 5 and sold at 100, but I would guess that this person's serious money portfolio did not do very well.

I am often asked questions like this: "I lost 25 percent of my money in a mutual fund retirement account. How do I recover that loss?" I would answer with this question: "If you bought a house today as an investment that you knew you weren't going to sell until retirement age, and the appraisal dropped 25 percent from where you bought it, what would you do?" You would probably buy more, but use a different realtor for advice. I formed Spectrum Financial for the express purpose of investing the money of family, friends, and clients the way I would invest my own. I would encourage anyone who may need investment help to refer to the resource section in the back of the book.

Protect your wealth with insurance. Insurance is an important protection against unexpected financial loss.

My basic philosophy on insurance is not to insure the small things that you can financially replace, but insure the things that are too big to replace. For example, use larger deductibles and self-insure whatever you can. Insure for a high amount with a larger deductible liability policy.

Disability insurance is the most important insurance for a wage earner who has not had time to accumulate assets. Many people would never think of not insuring their house and car, but if you lost your house or car, you could replace them if you still had an income. Income replacement due to loss of health is not possible to replace. If you had a goose that laid golden eggs, would you insure the eggs or the goose?

Life insurance is needed for families to insure adequate family income through the critical years of education, or maybe to pay estate taxes or other liabilities at death. The debate for term versus permanent insurance will go on forever, but my suggestion is to calculate how much you need, then figure out how much of the need is temporary (term) and how much is permanent (whole life) and get some of both.

Universal variable life insurance is a product that allows you to mix term insurance and whole life investment in one policy. Any extra funds that are paid into the policy in excess of the term cost will go directly to the investment account, which can be directed into an interest-bearing or stock or bond market investment account that will grow on a tax-favored basis.

Actually, life insurance is an efficient tool for passing wealth on from generation to generation. If properly arranged, it can be set up to avoid both income taxation and estate taxation at death. Many people could actually leave most of their assets to charity to avoid any estate taxes, and then "reforest" their estate with family-owned life insurance that may be passed tax-free to heirs at death. A qualified financial planner can assist you, particularly one who specializes in charitable estate planning. Anyone who may be subject to estate taxes should carefully consider this very creative area of planning. Estate taxes are not mandatory for a family with creative philanthropic planning techniques.

Consider charitable trusts. On my recommendation, my dad has set up a trust that benefits charity and pays income for ten years to his grandchildren during the time they will likely need funds most, during their early marriage years. He is making a gift of appreciated real estate to a charitable remainder trust that can sell it without paying any capital gains tax and invest the proceeds in income-producing stocks and bonds. His grandchildren receive income from the trust for 10 years. After 10 years, his favorite charity receives the balance in the trust. Each year, he gets an opportunity to talk to each of the grandchildren and advise them on how to invest the trust income they are receiving. Meanwhile, he receives an income tax deduction for the present calculated value of the charitable gift. He also removes the asset from being subject to estate taxes at his death. If he dies prior to the ten years, the trust continues to pay income to the grandchildren for the remainder of the ten-year period, and then the charity receives the remainder of the gift.

My dad gives while he is alive so he is able to see what happens with his gift, and he also has the opportunity to interact with his grandchildren every year. He gets both tax benefits and eternal benefits. On hearing about the plan, one granddaughter indicated her desire to take her entire first year payment and put it toward building a church in a Third World country. I jokingly told my dad that I want him to have a big mansion in Heaven because I will be coming to visit with all my kids. People have a tendency to keep on saving and investing until they die, and then leave it to their kids. There is an upper limit on what an individual can use in a lifetime. Decide how much is enough, then give the rest. Everyone with wealth will eventually make a charitable gift to someone—when they die. Be proactive. Give now.

How you handle your money affects your relationship with God. Jesus said, "If therefore you have not been faithful in handling worldly wealth, who will trust you with true riches?"[44] Jesus equates how we handle money with the quality of our spiritual life. If we handle money properly, according to Scripture, our fellowship with God will grow stronger. If we are not faithful with our money, our fellowship with Him will suffer. My children continue to remind me of the lesson I taught them: "Remember, Dad, it's not yours, it's God's."

40. Proverbs 11:24.

41. Malachi 3:10 NKJV.

42. Proverbs 21:5 TLB.

43. Proverbs 22:7.

44. Luke 16:11 NIV.

ELEVEN

FINISHING WELL

MY MOST PROSPEROUS PLAN EVER,
WITH ETERNAL BENEFITS,
CAME WHEN I ENTERED A
RELATIONSHIP WITH JESUS CHRIST
AND LET GOD RUN MY LIFE.

I've discovered that you can study about Jesus all your life and still not know Him. My awards for years of perfect attendance in Sunday School proved that. Knowing about someone is quite different from meeting and knowing Him. We meet Jesus through revelation, which is the work of the Holy Spirit within us. He reveals Himself to those who seriously seek Him and honestly look for Him.

155

IN GOD

As I seek Jesus, He gradually reveals Himself to me, and I experience Him. His love gives me freedom to choose to respond to Him in an ongoing relationship. He helps me to become the unique person that He intended me to be, and shows me how to accept others as the unique people that they are.

"But without faith it is impossible to please Him, for he who comes to God must believe that He is, and that He is a rewarder of those who diligently seek Him."[45]

THE DIFFERENCE HE HAS MADE IN MY LIFE

I remember one day as a teenager hearing someone talk about being baptized in the Holy Spirit. Although I was water baptized when I was ten years old, I asked my mom about it. My mom always seemed to have answers to my spiritual questions. She said something that I never forgot: "When it happens to you, you will know, but you will not understand it until then."

I tucked away that bit of information for future reference. Then, when I turned 30, I was at a Christian retreat for a week of prayer, worship, teaching, and soul searching. It happened. I had a personal encounter with Jesus. Before that it was all head knowledge. Now it was a VERY personal relationship.

I can only describe some of the changes in my life immediately after that:

My prayer life became powerful, not just superficial words.

Worship took on a new dimension. I looked for a church where praise and worship were emphasized, because in that environment I could hear God speak to me more clearly, a connection that I had never had before.

IN GOD

When I said the name of Jesus, my eyes would tear up. I now understood why He died for me, and that He was available for an ongoing relationship daily.

The Bible became alive, made sense to me, and was interesting. Words leaped off the page.

I received practical business insight that I never had before.

I was convicted of various kinds of sin in my life— slowly at first, then at an accelerating rate. Behavior that was once normal for me was no longer acceptable.

I had dreams that revealed things to me.

I discerned that evil spirits were real, not just fairytales.

God spoke to me every day, not just on Sundays.

Before this experience religion was rules, after this experience it was a relationship.

O.K., Mom. I understand now.

Never in my life could I have imagined the variety of situations and places in which I would become involved in the years to come. My life still continues to amaze me as I follow the leading of God. Major turning points in my life never came as the result of planning, but resulted from a small act of obedience toward something where I felt God was directing me.

Long after the fact I would see how His prompting had led me into another area of work or ministry.

As I have learned the benefits and excitement of obeying whatever God calls me to do, the phrase "Yes, Lord" has seemed less dangerous to say. Retirement? No way! Too boring! The dream of financial independence is a deceitful dream, but dependence on a God Who knows me better than I could know myself has become a place of rest from my former stormy, self-absorbed life.

SPIRITUAL GROWTH PROCESS

Spiritual growth involves a lifelong process:
- *Discovery of a truth* previously unknown.
- *Decisions to act on that truth,* leading to life change and spiritual maturity.

According to the teaching of the Bible, life on earth will have eternal consequences.
- *Our earthly belief* determines our eternal *destination.*
- *Our earthly behavior* determines our eternal *compensation.*

The Bible teaches us that "all have sinned and fallen short of the glory of God." [46] All of us have done or thought things that were not right. If we are honest with ourselves, we don't have a clear conscience. When we ask God to bring to our minds the things that are troubling us, we can confess them as wrong and ask for forgiveness. Because God is holy, He hates sin. Because He is just, He has arranged a way for us to be restored to a relationship with Him in spite of our sin, sending Jesus Christ to die in our place.

SIMPLE PRAYER WITH ETERNAL CONSEQUENCES

A simple prayer with eternal consequences can settle this issue for each one of us by asking God for forgiveness:

"God, Whoever you are, wherever You are, I need Your help. I am sorry for the mistakes I have made with my life. Thank You for sending Jesus to pay the penalty for me. Please forgive me and come into my life, and I will live for You now."

Pray this prayer with sincerity and watch your life change! Praying this prayer determines your eternal *destination* with God, but it is what you do (your works) after you become a believer that will determine your eternal *compensation*. Your actions as a manager of your life and God's resources will affect your eternal rewards.

Jesus was not being mystical when he talked about tangible rewards in the next life. He talked about

treasure—in this life and the next. He said that we could try to preserve our earthly treasures now, and fail, because we live in a fallen world where the system is corrupt. Or, we could follow His counsel to preserve treasure and send it on ahead—into heaven. Once there, it is secure, placed in the name of the person who sent it.

> JESUS SAID TO HIM, "IF YOU WANT TO BE PERFECT, GO, SELL WHAT YOU HAVE AND GIVE TO THE POOR, AND YOU WILL HAVE TREASURE IN HEAVEN; AND COME, FOLLOW ME."[47]

This concept of eternal treasures may seem like heresy to some churchgoers, but so many Scriptures back up this concept that it cannot be overlooked. If more people would take this concept literally, the Christian community would not have so much wealth parked in investment accounts, and charitable foundations would have more invested in God's *current* agenda.

Jesus' last words to us in Matthew 28:19 instruct us to go into all the world and preach the good news to every person, and make disciples of all nations. I am certain that a person's last words should have the greatest importance. They tend to summarize a person's life message. Maybe we need to contemplate Jesus' last words more often.

DIVERSIFIED INVESTMENT IN GOD'S WORK

I have chosen to give to causes that I feel are most effective in fulfilling His last words. I diversify my contributions among several organizations that are the best at doing what I call God's agenda. My list of diversified investments in God's work is listed in the Resource section in the back of this book.

These organizations present the Gospel, make disciples, build churches, train leaders, give to the poor, and heal the sick. By diversifying my portfolio of giving just as I do my investment portfolio, I am confident that these organizations are providing a significant return on my investment. More importantly, I feel that I am giving as God is directing me. Others will be led to support other people or organizations who are making a difference. What is important is that we remain open to God's leading in this area, since where we give is most often motivated by the heart. Now, when I receive any gift from God, I thank Him and ask a single question: "Since You have given me this new asset, is it to be used for sowing, or is it for me to use for a season?"

Don't Wait Too Long

Take a moment and inventory your assets. Do you have any seed in your barn that is just sitting there, inactive and unproductive? Jot down anything that comes to mind in the back of this book for future evaluation. Just don't wait too long. Life itself is a gift from God, and is more tenuous than most of us realize.

We all think we are going to live forever, as I discovered when I was selling life insurance. No one who bought it really thought that they would ever use it. Recently I experienced my first serious racing accident. Although I received a safe driving award last year, this time I rolled my car four times at about 80 miles per hour in a freak incident at the Porsche Club Enduro Race at Road America in Wisconsin. It's fresh in my mind that the time to start thinking about these things is not while you're flat on your back, an IV in your arm and a brace on your neck, with an ambulance attendant asking you if you remember your name.

I do remember you, Jeremy. Thanks for your help.

Thanks to adequate safety equipment, God has given me another opportunity to evaluate my giving plans, and my living plans. He took His car, but He left me here to do more work on behalf of others. Simon Wiesenthal, whose life was dedicated to bringing Nazis to justice, said "Survival is a privilege which entails obligations." My heart's desire is to make a difference and to encourage others to make one also. I want to be ready for the day, as in the parable of the master's talents, when the master came and said, "Well done, good and faithful servant! You have been faithful with a few things; I will put you in charge of many things. Come and share your master's happiness!"[48]

My Greatest Fulfillment

Someone asked a professor of psychology, "What is your greatest fulfillment as a professor?" He replied, "To help my students find a way whereby they can lose themselves and be themselves in the work they choose. I'm convinced that our vocation should be an extension of ourselves, and when a student finds work that challenges him and enables him to be himself, as a professor, I'm at my highest peak."

When I read the bestseller *The Purpose Driven Life* by Rick Warren, it opened up new ideas about the purpose of my life and answered many questions about where I was going. I had spent many years allowing selfish ambition to interfere with the more important, quality areas of my life, fighting with God about what I wanted to do and what I would become. I had wrong motives. I was selfish, greedy, and full of pride. I was not interested in addressing any of these issues, because I felt ashamed and guilty. Welcome to the human condition. I viewed God as being on one side and what I wanted on the other, until I realized that one of us was wrong.

Realizing that I was dealing with a God Who loved me was the first step.

Confessing my sinful nature and agreeing with God defused the issues of pride in my life and allowed God to begin changing me from the inside out. I am not stuck with "that's just the way I am" for the rest of my life. I wanted to fight God when I had a worldly vision of who I am. My value judgments came out of what I DO instead of who I AM. The quality of my life often depended on how the market performance was doing, or someone else's opinion of me. I began to realize that giving myself to God in the areas of my emotional needs created an environment for Him to change those areas.

Fighting a God who loves me is foolish. Dr. E. Stanley Jones once said, "Any time any believer gives everything they know about themselves to everything they know about God—watch out!" And Tommy Tyson said it this way: "God's will for you is exactly what you would choose for yourself if you had sense enough to know." God wants to work with us like the professor helping his students to find their highest

calling. If only I will slow down now and listen more carefully since every decision I make now will have an eternal consequence.

> *"And as [Aslan] spoke, He no longer looked to them like a lion; but the things that began to happen after that were so great and beautiful I cannot write them. And for us this is the end of all the stories, and we can most truly say that they lived happily ever after. But for them it was only the beginning of the real story. All their life in this world and all their adventures in Narnia had only been the cover and the title page: now at last they were beginning Chapter One of the Great Story which no one on earth has read: which goes on for ever: in which every chapter is better than the one before."*[49]

45. Hebrews 11:6 NKJV.

46. Romans 3:23.

47. Matthew 19:21 NKJV.

48. Matthew 25:21 NIV.

49. C. S. Lewis, *The Last Battle*. In C. S. Lewis, *The Chronicles of Narnia* (New York: HarperCollins Publishers, 2001), p. 767.

RESOURCES AND NOTES

AUTHOR'S WEBSITES

WEALTH CONUNDRUM WEBSITE
HTTP://WEALTHCONUNDRUM.COM

This site was designed by the author to help you put your financial puzzle in better perspective. Resources and links include ministries supported by the author, biblical stewardship of money, spiritual growth, fellowships of givers, financial management, gift and estate design, and book orders for *Wealth Conundrum* by Ralph J. Doudera.

SPECTRUM FINANCIAL WEBSITE
HTTP://SPECTRUMFIN.COM

Ralph J. Doudera is CEO of Spectrum Financial Inc., a Registered Investment Advisor (since 1988) that actively manages client investment portfolios by using a wide array of investment strategies. These strategies are designed to help investors achieve performance with peace of mind. Spectrum's investment philosophy is founded on the principle that the use of multiple actively managed strategies is the best time-tested way to achieve above average returns with below average risk.

Spectrum Financial, Inc., 2940 N. Lynnhaven Rd., Suite 200, Virginia Beach, VA 23452
Office (888) 463-7600, (757) 463-7600
Fax (757) 463-1232

Author's Giving Portfolio

Note from Ralph Doudera

The following organizations are part of my current personal investment portfolio for giving. They are diversified, yet effective in utilizing a multiplication factor in various strategies. These are only a few of many effective ministries. I diversify my contributions to the organizations listed below because to me they are among the best at doing what I call God's agenda.

Haggai Institute for Advanced Leadership Training
www.haggai-institute.com

Since 1969, HI has provided advanced leadership skills for evangelism to more than 55,000 leaders in 175 nations, nearly all non-western. Each graduate commits to training at least 100 more people—nationals training nationals. This is an exponential multiplication of investment in people similar to the way that cash investments grow with compound interest. Only faster.

The JESUS Film Project
WWW.JESUSFILM.ORG

This organization distributes the film JESUS, a two-hour docu-drama about the life of Christ based on the Gospel of Luke. Since its release in 1979, the film has been seen in every country of the world and translated into hundreds of languages, conveying the message of Jesus Christ to people in their own language in a simple, profound way.

International Cooperating Ministries
WWW.ICM.ORG

ICM gives and loans funds to build churches in the Third World and provides study materials for Bible colleges in many languages. Funds that are repaid are loaned out again to build more churches and provide more discipleship and leadership materials, nurturing believers and assisting church growth.

Opportunity International
WWW.OPPORTUNITY.ORG

This organization offers micro-loan financing to poor entrepreneurs in emerging countries, providing employment for many families. By loaning the money to small syndicates, Opportunity International has been able to obtain a high payback rate. The proceeds are recycled to fund new participants. This helps the poor to become self-sufficient.

CURE International
WWW.CUREINTERNATIONAL.ORG

CURE builds and operates teaching hospitals for the medical and spiritual healing of disabled children and their families in the

developing world. This Christian outreach is committed to evangelism, excellence, and long-term sustainability, including the training of national surgeons.

LOCAL COMMUNITY NEEDS

Giving to local needs keeps me in touch with my community, and my tithe goes to my local church.

BIBLICAL STEWARDSHIP OF MONEY

CROWN FINANCIAL MINISTRIES
WWW.CROWN.ORG

The goals of Crown Financial Ministries are to equip people worldwide to learn, apply, and teach God's financial principles for achieving financial freedom. Check out their outstanding resources for personal financial planning.

ETERNAL PERSPECTIVE MINISTRIES
WWW.EPM.ORG

The objectives of Eternal Perspective Ministries are to teach the principles of God's Word, emphasizing an eternal viewpoint, and to reach the needy.

SPIRITUAL GROWTH

PURPOSE DRIVEN LIFE
WWW.PURPOSEDRIVENLIFE.COM

Purpose Driven Life is committed to helping people on the journey of finding and living a better life full of purpose. The website provides tools and resources to connect people with others on the same journey.

Camps Farthest Out

WWW.ACFONA.ORG

Camps Farthest Out (CFO) is a nondenominational Christian organization dedicated to helping people grow in their faith. CFO offers an environment where people can step out of a frantic life and tune in to God.

Fellowship Groups Of Givers

Generous Giving

WWW.GENEROUSGIVING.ORG

Generous Giving is a privately funded ministry that seeks to encourage givers of all income levels—ministry leaders, pastors, teachers, and professional advisors—to experience the joy of giving and embrace a lifestyle of generosity.

Ministry of Money

WWW.MINISTRYOFMONEY.ORG

Ministry of Money creates opportunities for women and men from all walks of life to explore their own personal relationship to money from a faith perspective.

The Gathering

WWW.THEGATHERING.COM

These are people engaged in Christian philanthropy who are looking for like-minded individuals to serve as a sounding board of peers, an information resource, and a source of spiritual encouragement.

IN GOD   WE TRUST

Estate and Gift Design

Calvin Edwards & Company
http://www.calvinedwardscompany.com

These advisors provide impartial information and advice based on client-defined criteria.

Excellence in Giving
http://www.excellenceingiving.com/Home.aspx

This is a full service philanthropic service firm that helps potential donors to focus their giving.

Portell Financial Services
www.portellfs.com

Provides creative solutions in the accumulation, conservation and distribution of net worth.

National Center for Family Philanthropy
http://www.ncfp.org/

This organization promotes philanthropic values, vision, and excellence across generations of donors and donor families.

Ron Blue &Company
http://www.ronblue.com

This company offers fee-only financial and investment management services to over 5,000 clients through 14 offices across the U.S.

ADDITIONAL READING

Alcorn, Randy. *Money, Possessions and Eternity.* Carol Stream, Illinois: Tyndale House, 2003.

Alcorn, Randy. *The Treasure Principle.* Sisters, Oregon: Multnomah Publishing, 2001.

Avanzini, Dr. John. *Rich God, Poor God.* Tulsa, Oklahoma: Abel Press, 2001.

Dayton, Howard. *Your Money Counts. The biblical guide to earning, spending, saving, investing, giving and getting out of debt.* Gainesville, Georgia: Crown Financial Ministries, 1996.

Foster, Richard. *Freedom of Simplicity.* San Francisco: HarperSanFrancisco, 1998.

Wilkinson, Bruce. *A Life God Rewards: Why Everything You Do Today Matters Forever* (Breakthrough Series Bk. 3). Sisters, Oregon: Multnomah Publishing, 2002.

IN GOD   WE TRUST

ABOUT THE AUTHOR

RALPH J. DOUDERA is the CEO of Spectrum Financial Inc., a registered investment advisory firm in Virginia Beach, Virginia, and has been responsible for investing hundreds of millions of dollars of client assets since 1987. He also serves as advisor to Hundredfold Advisors LLC, which provides investment advisory services to three diversified mutual funds. His past investment strategies have provided above average returns while reducing market risk. He has contributed millions of dollars to solve global issues related to the Great Commission for Christian evangelism, world poverty, leadership training, and church building. He holds degrees in Mechanical Engineering, Management and Finance, and Biblical Studies. His hobbies include the Porsche Club of America Racing program, surfing (at his hotel in Costa Rica), photography, and composing and recording music and video. He is married to his wife Tara, and has a son, five daughters, and three grandchildren.

PERSONAL NOTES